DEBORAH

DEBORAH

By

Margit Strom Heppenstall

Southern
Publishing
Association
Nashville
Tennessee

ISBN 8127-0169-0

Library of Congress Catalog Card Number: 67-19497

Cover painting by Bill Myers

Design by Peter Erhard

Printed in U.S.A.

Dedication

To three very special girls, Kathleen, Susan, and Barbara, with love from "Aunt" Margit.

Contents

1

CAPTURED!

Afterward, when it was too late, Deborah knew she had been foolish and careless. If she had only heeded her mother's warning! If she had only not wanted her own way!

"Oh, Mother," she had begged that lovely spring morning, "please let me go into the hills and pick some flowers. The rains have made everything pretty and fresh, and I haven't been anywhere for so long. Nothing ever happens here. I want some fun."

"No, Deborah; it isn't safe. Bands of Syrian soldiers are raiding the neighborhood again. I can't let you go."

"But, Mother, they wouldn't come this far south of the border. Besides, Tirzah can go with me. I wouldn't be all alone."

"Tirzah? An empty-headed servant girl only a year older than you—what help would she be?" Mother shook her head and turned back to her spinning. "Besides, Tirzah has work to do. No, you will have to wait until your father and your brothers can go with you."

"That will never be," muttered Deborah under her breath. "They never have time. Work, work, work—that's all we do in this house. What do we have servants for, I wonder." Her face wore a scowl as she sighed and gazed wistfully at the tempting hills in the distance.

Her mother took in the situation at a glance. "No use feeling sorry for yourself, Deborah. You're better off than other girls I might mention. The God of our fathers has blessed us with prosperity. You didn't have to work when you were little as so many do. You've had your years of play. But now that you are ten, you must grow up. You must learn to cook and sew and spin and weave. So go back to your loom and forget about your foolish ideas."

Seeing the stormy look in Deborah's eyes, she softened her words with a smile and added, "You know I love you too much to let you go where danger may hide. Believe me, it is for the best."

However, as the day wore on, Deborah did not forget her wish. Often her shuttle would stop or move reluctantly across the warp of the linen cloth she was designing on the simple loom in the courtyard. As she looked up at the bright sky and felt the breeze from the mountains tousle the dark curls around her forehead, a rather daring plan formed in her mind.

After the noonday meal of lentils, curdled milk, and bread from the morning's baking, she managed to get Tirzah into a corner. "How would you like to go into the hills with me and pick wild poppies? We can go while the others are taking their afternoon rest."

Tirzah's sullen face took on a look of suspicion. She flung her straight black hair away from her shoulders and dug her toes into the dust of the courtyard before answering. "Why do you want to go then? Did your mother say you couldn't go?"

Deborah nodded. "She has some strange idea that it would be too dangerous. She says Syrian soldiers have been seen roaming around. But it's only a rumor. Besides, you know how fast you and I can run if we see anybody coming. Let's go, Tirzah! We've worked enough for a while!"

"That may be all right for you, but I'm not free to decide. I'm only a slave, remember?" Tirzah's lower lip shot out defiantly as she almost spit out the hated word. "If anyone finds out, your father will beat me as he did when we let the doves out the other day. And it was really your fault. I don't want to go with you."

"Then I shall have to remind you that when your father had to sell you to pay his debt, you were bought to be my own servant. I'm *telling* you to come with me! And if there's any trouble, I promise that this time I'll take all the blame." Her voice changed quickly from command to persuasion. "Mother's going to see Josiah's sick wife this afternoon. She will not be here when we leave. We'll be back in time to help fix supper. Come on, Tirzah. We'll have a wonderful time. You won't be sorry."

"You won't be sorry!" Those words were to echo in Deborah's mind and sting her like poisoned arrows. But that was later—when it was too late.

To begin with they did have a wonderful time. When they first slipped down the narrow alley to the city gate, Deborah felt some twinges of conscience for her disobedience. But soon they were outside the walls, climbing like two goats up the gentle grassy slopes. Here she forgot her qualms for the sheer joy of being alive. The first swallows were wheeling joyously about in the keen-edged spring air.

"Look, Tirzah, I can fly, too," Deborah shouted, all out of breath, as she reached the top of the first hill. She gathered the hem of her cloak in her hands and stretched out her arms to form a pair of make-believe black wings. Then she rushed down the hill with the breeze at her back, squealing with glee. Up and down she went, until she flung herself tired and happy by Tirzah's side. The older girl, content with less strenuous exercise, had found a patch of poppies and was picking them listlessly.

Deborah filled her hands with the bright blossoms. "Um-m-m, isn't this perfect? And what a view! Jabesh-gilead, with its strong walls and towers, looks like an important city from here. And look way to the north! That white must be the snow on Mount Hermon. I had forgotten how far you can see from here on a clear day."

She lay down on her stomach, resting her chin in her cupped hands. Her brown eyes roved over the vista spread before them. "How beautiful the Jordan Valley is in the spring! Look, Tirzah; up near the Sea of Chinnereth there's Mount Tabor where Deborah and Barak gathered the tribes of Israel to fight against Jabin and Sisera. Father has told me the story many times. I'm glad he named me for that great Deborah. I guess I'll never be as famous as she was. But I would like to do something for the Lord. It's fun to dream about it. Maybe I'll marry into an important family as Ruth did. Or maybe I'll become the mother of a great man, like Hannah, the mother of Samuel. What do you dream about, Tirzah?"

The next instant Deborah knew those words would have been better left unspoken. Tirzah gave her a venomous look and muttered, "Dream? Slaves don't dream! Or didn't you know that?"

"But you won't always be a slave. After seven years you may go out free if you wish." Deborah was trying to smooth things over, but she succeeded only in making them worse.

"If I wish!" Tirzah's laugh was bitter. "Seven years is a long time. I might be dead before then."

Deborah looked in amazement at her companion. Tirzah was not an attractive girl at best. Her matted black hair hung straight to her shoulders, framing a bony face with a large nose and small eyes, beady and black like those of a snake. Her hands and feet were too large and always seemed to be getting in her way. With the ugly expression on her face right now she looked downright repulsive.

Deborah shuddered and sprang to her feet. "Come, let's go over to that other hill. Joel told me there is a better view from there. I'm sure I see more flowers on the other slope, too."

So midafternoon found the two girls on a hillside some distance from the protection of the city's watchtowers. Jabesh in Gilead was an important town in the province of Israel, which bordered on Syria. But the closeness of the enemy land was far away from Deborah's thoughts as she admired her large bouquet of spring flowers. She felt her eyes growing heavy in the warm sunshine, and she said, "It's too hot to wear a cloak. Here, I'll spread mine on the grass. We have time to rest awhile before we go home."

She did not intend to go to sleep. She only wanted to close her eyes for a moment and drink in the fragrance of the air and the earth, throbbing with newly awakened life.

But when she was aroused with a start after what seemed only a twinkling of time, the sun was low in the west. Rough voices shouted around her. Strong arms grabbed her and held her fast. She tried to scream in order to break the spell of what she knew must be a nightmare, a horrible dream. But a rough hand slapped across her mouth and stifled her cry for help, a cry that would have fallen far short of reaching any sympathetic ear.

Deborah blinked her eyes wildly. Waves of fear engulfed

her. Cold terror twisted her stomach into a tight knot. The rosy light of the sinking sun glinted on helmets and swords. There could be no doubt. Unhappily, this was no dream, no fantasy. The men who had surprised her and Tirzah while they slept were the Syrian soldiers mother had warned her about. This was no mere rumor. This was all too real. In a flash she recalled the horrible tales she had heard about these enemies and what they did to their captives.

"Why did I disobey mother?" she thought. "What will happen to us now? They'll kill us!"

She glanced around the circle of men. There were about ten, a rough-looking lot with short beards and leathery faces. Two of them held Tirzah, who was squirming and kicking like a wildcat. One of the other soldiers quickly raised his short sword.

Deborah found her voice again. Her captor, realizing that they were too far from the city to be heard by anyone, had dropped his hand from her lips. "No, no!" She almost choked on the words with the fierce pounding of her heart in her throat. "Don't kill her! Let us go! My father is Heber, a merchant of Jabesh-gilead. He is an important man. If you let us go, he will reward you well!"

The men burst into raucous laughter.

"Sure, little maid; and how would we collect the reward without having the entire garrison in Jabesh-gilead on our heels? No, we have other plans for you. But you two better behave yourselves, or you won't like what might happen to you." So spoke the leader of the band, a tall fellow with a perpetual sneer curling his lips. He made a gesture as if drawing an imaginary dagger across his throat. The men laughed uproariously again.

Tirzah started to sob. The two men holding her let her

drop back on the grass beside Deborah and stood aside to survey their frightened captives.

"Not bad, huh, Massa?" one of them said to the leader. "A valuable catch, and as easily taken as two ripe figs tumbling into my hands."

Massa nodded. "They both look healthy. If the little one tells the truth about coming from a high-class home, she'll bring a good price in Damascus. With that pink skin and dark hair and those eyes like a fawn, she might be pretty enough for a prince when she grows up."

"Too bad the other one is so plain," another added. "But if she'll stand the trip, we'll get a fair price for her also. Let's be on our way. We must make camp before dark."

Deborah wanted to say something to Tirzah, but the soldiers separated them and hurried them down the hill through a rocky ravine to the north. As she stumbled along, Deborah sneaked a glance over her shoulder. Down there behind the hills was Jabesh, and home. Maybe at this very moment her mother had returned to the house to prepare the evening meal. Maybe right now she was calling through the courtyard, "Deborah! Deborah! Where are you?"

Her father and Joel and Ira would be gathering the neighbors to go out and search for her. But it would be too late. It would soon be dark, with no hope of successful pursuit.

"Why, oh, why did this have to happen to me?" she asked herself. But she knew the answer only too well.

The sun set. In the long twilight the band of soldiers hustled the two young captives without mercy up and down the rugged hills. The girls stumbled, fell, and were dragged to their feet again while the soldiers swore angrily. Deborah's feet were bleeding, and her head throbbed. It was almost a relief when at last they reached a cave in a desert mountain. Here a campfire blazed, cleverly hidden from view. Several soldiers rested by it, watching a large pot which smelled of meat cooking.

"They steal sheep as well as people," thought Deborah with contempt.

When her eyes got used to the smoke and darkness of the rock shelter, she could make out another group of captives huddled in the back of the cave. She wanted to join them, but the soldiers motioned for her to sit on the other side of the fire. Exhausted, she sank down beside Tirzah, hoping to find some consolation from the only other familiar face there. She was almost too numb with despair and fatigue to observe anything around her. But she noticed with surprise a strange look of triumph in her slave girl's eyes as she whispered to her, "Tirzah, I'm sorry. This is all my fault. Please forgive me! I wish I could do something to help you, but I can't."

"Sorry, indeed!" hissed Tirzah. "Well, this serves you right. Now you'll find out what it's like to be a slave. As for me, what does it matter? Being a slave in Syria can't be much worse than being a slave in the tribe of Gad. At least you can't order me around anymore. You know something, Deborah? I hate you! I've hated you every moment since I came to live at your house."

Deborah recoiled as though Tirzah had struck her. This was too much. She turned away and flung herself down on a piece of cloth on the ground. Then she recognized it as her own cloak which the soldiers had brought along—her cloak, made of wool from her favorite sheep; carded, spun, and lovingly woven by her mother!

"Mother!" cried her heart in agitation and anguish. Now,

at last, the tears welled up in her eyes like a flood. She must not, she would not, let Tirzah see her cry. She crawled toward the darkest corner of the cave and lay down, wrapping the cloak around her. Then, stuffing one of the sleeves into her mouth to stifle the sound of her sobbing, Deborah cried herself to sleep.

2

A New Friend

When Deborah awoke hours later, it was still dark. For a moment she did not remember where she was or what had happened. Then it all came back to her in a wave of horror. The foul-smelling cave made her sick. Her eyes and throat were sore from crying and from the sour smoke, which still curled up from the embers of the dying fire. But the ache in her heart was even worse than these discomforts.

"I'd give anything to be back home again," she thought. "I would work and work and never complain, no matter what mother asked me to do. I would never disobey her again as long as I lived! Now I'll never see her again. I can't even tell her how sorry I am and ask her to forgive me. Poor mother and father and Joel and Ira—they must be worried about me. They will guess what happened, but there's nothing they can do. They could never find me here. What will happen to me? I feel like Tirzah. I wish I were dead, too!"

The thought of Tirzah and her ugly words brought the tears to her eyes again, but she fought them back. "Mother always said not to cry over something that can't be helped. She said to make the best of everything even when I didn't feel like it. But how can I make the best of this? Even God has forsaken me."

Deborah studied the huddled figures of the soldiers and

their captives, all seemingly asleep. The mouth of the cave framed a patch of the night sky, alive with twinkling stars. She felt a wild hope trembling within her as she crept noiselessly toward the fresh air.

"Maybe I can find my way back if I can only get outside and decide which way is south and west. Father has taught us a lot about the stars. I think I can do it. I'm going to try."

She made her way like a shadow past the figures on the floor. Once she stopped, petrified, when someone sneezed and turned over. She waited, without daring to breathe, until she realized that no one's sleep had been disturbed. After what seemed an eternity, she stood outside.

The cleanness of the night air greeted her like a benediction. She drank it in for a moment, studying the stars to get her bearings. "There is the North Star. Then home is down that way. Quiet now, not a sound. Oh, these rocks are slippery. What if those loose stones start to roll?"

She felt her way cautiously in the dark, a few steps at a time. Then she stopped suddenly. There was a slight sound somewhere behind her like a crunching of pebbles. Was she being followed? Her heart beat so loudly that she imagined the whole world would be awakened by its pounding. She stood perfectly still.

"Where do you think you're going?" whispered a voice in her ear. "Do you want to get yourself killed?"

Deborah whirled around. She half expected to see a soldier with a raised sword ready to strike her down. Great was her relief to discover that it was only a boy, two or three years older than she. He dragged her into the shelter of a large boulder.

"Look down there." He pointed to a shadowy figure pacing back and forth halfway down the hill. "There are guards all around us. Did you think they would take a chance on anyone escaping? If they find you trying, they'll whip you to within a hand's breadth of your life."

Deborah stared at him. By now she could make out his face. He was a stocky, muscular lad with strong features under a shock of dark curly hair.

"How do you know?" she stammered. "Did they do that to you?"

The boy nodded and continued, "You're pretty brave for a girl, but you wouldn't live through what I had to take. You better get back into the cave before anyone misses you. They'll wake us up before dawn to get an early start."

Deborah made a face. "I'm not going back into that horrible-smelling cave. I'll lie down right by the door. Then they won't suspect anything."

The boy shrugged. "Suit yourself. I'll see you in the morning. But no one must know you came out here. Remember that."

With this warning he disappeared like a shadow. Deborah wrapped her cloak tightly around her against the chill of the night. She sat down by the cave opening and looked up at the stars. The fresh air gave her sinking spirits a lift, even though her hope of escape was shattered. The boy had been friendly in his gruff way. She no longer felt completely alone. Someone was concerned about her.

The stars twinkled at her as if they wanted to say, "We are your friends, too, Deborah. The same God who made us made you. He has not forsaken you. He is with you and will watch over you. Has He not spared your life twice already? Trust in Him, and it shall be well with you."

Deborah took a deep breath. A ray of hope stole into her tortured mind.

"The Lord is still with me," she thought. "I don't understand how, but I must believe. That is what father always says."

She bowed her head and whispered in the darkness, "Oh, Lord God of my fathers, God of Abraham, Isaac, and Jacob, look on me in mercy and forgive my sin of disobedience. I have no sacrifice to bring nor any place to bring it. But go with me and help me someday to get back home again!"

She remembered the words her father used to repeat when the family was seated together in the evening before going to bed. Her brothers had to memorize the words, and she had listened enough times so that they were indelibly engraved in her own heart:

"The Lord, The Lord God, merciful and gracious, long-suffering, and abundant in goodness and truth, keeping mercy for thousands, forgiving iniquity and transgression and sin, and that will by no means clear the guilty."

Peace filled Deborah's soul. She knew she was to blame for her misfortune, but at least God had forgiven her.

She thought of the story of Joseph, another of her father's favorites. "He was sold as a slave, too, and by his own brothers. That was even worse than what happened to me. But he didn't give up his faith in God. He determined to always do what was right; therefore God was with him, and God blessed him. That is my only hope, too. I have been a naughty girl, selfish and thoughtless. I've wanted my own way too much. Dear God, help me to be good and do what is right."

Thus Deborah thought and prayed in her loneliness and despair. In the star-studded hours before dawn she received strength she had never known about, for she had not needed it before. So, with peace and comfort in her heart at last, she lay down and fell asleep once more under the protecting wings of angels whom she could not see. But she knew they were there.

Before the first glow of dawn tinted the desert hills, the soldiers had marshaled their band of captives and were herding them north toward the Syrian border. Massa was taking no chances of being followed and overtaken. As Deborah and the other unfortunate kidnap victims put mile after weary mile between themselves and their homes, any hope of rescue died a lingering death.

With the coming of daylight Deborah had an opportunity to see the other captured Israelites. She saw no one there from her own town of Jabesh-gilead. Besides a number of older girls and some haggard-looking women, she noticed only two men. They were both past middle age and did not seem strong enough to stand the rigorous journey.

The boy whom she had met in the early morning was walking a few paces ahead of her. She wished he would turn around and speak to her, but there was no chance during the forced march. The ugly whip marks on his bare back reminded her of what he had said about the fate of those who tried to escape. He had evidently not been easily tamed by his captors, for there was still a proud lift to his chin. But he hurried along without murmuring. It was clear that he had no desire to risk any new acquaintance with the lash, which came down without mercy on the shoulders of those who found it hard to keep moving.

"Will this never end?" thought Deborah. "No supper last night and no time to eat this morning. If they intend to get us to Syria alive, they have a strange way of doing it."

Her stomach screamed with hunger, but her thirst was even worse as they made their way up and down the desert hills and gorges. The day was sultry, and finally a violent thunderstorm forced the soldiers to halt. They let everybody find shelter as best they could under an overhanging cliff. While resting, they passed out some parched corn and a few dried figs.

Deborah devoured her share greedily and cupped her hands to catch a drink from the rain that came pelting down. Tirzah had not spoken to her all morning, but she was willing to huddle with Deborah under her cloak when it was offered. She cowered in fear when the lightning struck rocks on the other side of the ravine and sent them crashing down. The Syrians fell on their faces and mumbled prayers to Rimmon, their god of thunder.

Tirzah finally found her tongue. "I hate thunder and lightning," she whispered. "Praying to Rimmon is not going to do us any good. Baal is the true god of storm and rain. Maybe he is angry and will kill us with his shafts of fire."

It was hard for Deborah to remember that she was no longer Tirzah's mistress. She began reproachfully, "Why, Tirzah, you must not——" but quickly corrected herself, "I mean, you know that in our house we believe that the Lord God of Israel sends the thunder and the rain. He is the only true God. How can Baal or Rimmon, who are made of wood or brass, have power to make a storm like this? Only God can do that. It is His voice we hear in the thunder."

There was a sudden movement behind them. "If your God is so powerful, why did He let you be taken by the Syrians? Surely that proves that either Baal or Rimmon is mightier than Jahve," said a voice she thought she recognized.

She turned around. There stood the boy she had wanted to talk to again. His body and loincloth were soaked with rain. His proud eyes had a defiant look.

Deborah's heart sank. She had hoped he might be a

believer in the true God. But she rose to the challenge. "Didn't you ever hear about the time when the prophet Elijah made the great test by fire on Mount Carmel? He proved then that Baal is no god and that the Lord is the only true God. Who are you, anyway?"

"I am Ethan, the son of Uriah, from Bethel. My father and I were on a trading journey in Gilead when the Syrians overtook us. They killed my father when he tried to resist, and here I am," he concluded grimly. "My mother died two years ago, so no one is looking for me."

"I'm sorry." Deborah's face clouded over. "He must have been a brave man. I am Deborah, daughter of Heber, of the tribe of Gad. My home is in Jabesh-gilead. This is Tirzah, my—companion," she finished up rather awkwardly.

"I used to be her handmaiden," volunteered Tirzah. "Now we are equal!" She giggled maliciously.

Ethan sensed the tension between the two girls. "I know the story of Elijah," he said quickly. "But that happened a long time ago. Baal is still being worshiped by many in Israel. Are you sure that the Lord God of Elijah has not forsaken us? He hasn't helped you much, has he?"

"It was my own fault that Tirzah and I were captured. I'm being punished because I disobeyed my mother. But I still believe that the Lord God is powerful in Israel. You've heard of the mighty miracles of the prophet Elisha?"

"Stop!" shouted Ethan, his face distorted with anger. "Don't mention that name to me again! I hate the prophet Elisha!"

Deborah turned pale with horror. "Ethan, you don't know what you're saying," she gasped. "You mustn't talk like that about God's prophet. Why do you hate him so?"

There was great bitterness in his voice as he replied, "Did

you ever hear of the young men who were cursed by the prophet outside the city of Bethel? You know, they were killed by wild bears from the woods, all forty-two of them."

"Yes, but——"

"One of them was my older brother. Now do you understand why I feel the way I do?"

"But, Ethan, they deliberately mocked the prophet of God. We know God will not allow that. That's the same as mocking the Lord Himself. There are some things the Lord will not overlook. Remember the story of Uzzah? He was struck dead for just touching the ark of the covenant. He didn't mean to be disrespectful. He thought he needed only to steady it on a rough road. But God had told His people never to touch the sacred ark, so Uzzah died. I am sorry about your brother, but you must admit that he ought to have known better."

Ethan stared at her, speechless. Then he crept out from his rocky shelter and half slid, half stumbled down the hill to where the soldiers were assembling the captives again to resume the march.

Deborah sighed as she and Tirzah followed. "I wish he would let me tell him about all the good and gentle things the prophet Elisha has done. The stories of his deeds have traveled all over Israel. He healed the bitter waters of Jericho and helped three kings defeat the Moabites. He made oil in the widow's vessels so that she would not have to sell her sons to pay her husband's debts."

"Too bad he couldn't have done the same for me. I wouldn't be here today," Tirzah interrupted sarcastically.

"Too bad your father didn't send for him and ask him to," retorted Deborah softly.

Tirzah hung her head. Her family worshiped Baal. This

time she was stumped for one of her usual sour replies, so she remained silent.

"The greatest miracle of them all," continued Deborah unabashed, "was when Elisha raised from the dead the little son of the woman of Shunem. If only Ethan would listen to some of these stories, maybe he would change his mind. I'm not going to give up yet."

3

The Slave Market

"There is Damascus!" the Syrian soldiers shouted joyfully when they and their captives scaled the last hill of the desert and caught sight of the valley of the Abana straight ahead. Some of them began chanting prayers of thanks to their gods for bringing them safely home with their rich booty. Now the reward was within their grasp.

Deborah nudged Tirzah. "Isn't it beautiful?"

Even to a captive approaching the enemy capital, Damascus was a lovely sight. The city was surrounded on all sides by green fields and orchards. With its limestone palaces and whitewashed houses gleaming in the sun, it looked like a pearl lying in a cup of emeralds. Three rivers—Abana, Pharpar, and Barada—watered the fertile plateau. The snow on the summits of the Anti-Lebanon range to the northwest was a striking contrast to the waving palms and blossoming pomegranate trees on the slopes below. A wave of fragrance from a thousand gardens filled the air. After the march through the barren wilderness with nothing but sand and sun-scorched rocks, the scene was doubly inviting. Still, it also held unknown terrors for the prisoners.

Tirzah said nothing, but Ethan, who was walking along with the two girls, spoke up. "Yes, it is beautiful, but what will happen to us now? Have you forgotten that soon we'll be sold in the slave market? If a kind master buys you, that's good. But if he is a cruel man, your life won't be worth a potsherd. I've seen too many slaves beaten to death, even in Israel."

"I believe the Lord will watch over us if we ask Him to," replied Deborah, trying to be brave. But her cheeks were pale under her suntan as she thought about what Ethan had said. "God helped Joseph in Egypt, even though he had many troubles. He can help us, too."

"You still believe that? My, my, aren't you the brave one!" mocked Tirzah.

Ethan was silent. Deborah had screwed up her courage to talk to him several times after their conversation during the thunderstorm. He still didn't want to hear anything about the prophet Elisha and his miracles, which were such a source of comfort to Deborah. But he didn't seem to object to the story of the slave boy who became prime minister of Egypt.

"Yes, I do believe," was Deborah's reply. "I'm not brave at all. I'm just as frightened as you are. But I hope that thinking about Joseph and what God did for him will at least help me not to show how frightened I am."

Ethan nodded. "I'm determined that those Syrian dogs are not going to have any good reason for making fun of me."

When they were marched in triumph through the city a short time later, the inhabitants of Damascus needed no particular reason for bursting into peals of scornful laughter at the sight of the captives. Deborah felt her cheeks burning with shame, but she looked straight ahead, refusing to acknowledge the rude remarks of the crowd with even a glance. She noticed that Ethan, who was in front of her, had lifted his chin to an even prouder angle than usual.

Before they were taken to the slave market, the prisoners were allowed to rest for a few days in a compound on the outskirts of the city. This was not because of any sudden kindness on the part of their captors. But the slaves would obviously sell for a better price after having time to bathe, groom their hair, and eat some good meals. Oils and ointments were given to them to heal the cuts and bruises of the journey. Each slave was also furnished with a clean tunic if his own garments were too worn to be used any longer. After three days it was difficult to recognize the tattered, sunburned prisoners who had dragged themselves wearily through the streets to the jeers of the mob.

Rested and refreshed, Deborah became more cheerful. On the day Massa took the captives to the marketplace, she looked about at some of the sights of the ancient city. After all, it was going to be her home.

To a girl from a small country town Damascus was a fascinating place. Some parts of it looked much the same as her hometown. The narrow, crooked streets, littered with filth of every description, were only too familiar. The flies and the unpleasant odors were part of the atmosphere and were taken for granted. But there was more excitement here, as traders from all over the East passed through with their caravans. There was the donkey market, and the spice market with its mysterious aroma of faraway lands. There were little food stalls along the banks of brooks running through the middle of the city. Shops of all kinds lined the streets, and Deborah's eyes were especially drawn to the open windows, through which she could see weavers at their looms, making the beautiful patterned silk cloth for which Damascus was famous. Street vendors chanted and shouted while they hawked their wares from house to house. A thirsty customer might buy a drink of water or milk or wine straight from a goatskin bag dangling on the back of a small boy. Sweets, pastries, and dried fruits were piled on the cobblestones and on the tables of open-air markets.

"How I would love some honey cakes sprinkled with coriander seeds!" thought Deborah.

"Halt! Keep your places in line!"

Massa's shout interrupted Deborah's dreaming. With a start she realized that they had reached their destination, an open square next to the city wall. Small wooden platforms had been erected to display the slaves. A large group of customers stood in the center of the marketplace.

"Oh, Tirzah," whispered Deborah, "this is awful. I hate to stand up there for everyone to look at as if I were an animal or something."

Tirzah sneered. "From now on you'll have to do a lot of things you don't like, young lady. Look at all those people. I wonder who'll buy us? See that fat fellow with the red-fringed cloak? He's got the meanest-looking face I've seen in a long time——"

"Sh-h!" warned Ethan in front of them. "Massa is looking this way. You're not supposed to be talking."

The girls clammed up. But Deborah's eyes strayed to the man Tirzah had described. He was fat to the point of discomfort, with large rolls of pink flesh where his neck and chin should have been. His round face was clean-shaven, and he might have looked almost pleasant except for the cruel expression on his thick lips and the cold look in his little piglike eyes. That look sent shivers through Deborah's very bones. A feeling of horrible premonition took hold of her. What if this man should buy her? What would happen to her then?

The auction began. The older slaves were displayed first. It soon became clear to Deborah that not all in the crowd were buyers. Most of them were onlookers who had come for whatever fun they could get out of it. A professional slave merchant was in charge of the selling, and he was doing his best to praise his wares.

"What am I bid," he shouted, "for this fine, strong Israelite? This woman can spin and weave the finest linen and cook excellent meals. She has a meek disposition and will work hard and eat little. A good investment! What am I bid?"

"She looks more like a skinny old goat than a woman," hooted someone in the mob. "She'd better have a good disposition to make up for it." The crowd howled with laughter.

Deborah's heart ached for the woman. She had learned her story during the long trip and knew that she had been the wife of a peasant and mistress of her own home, humble though it was. She had been kidnapped by the Syrians while she was out hoeing in the field. After much haggling between the auctioneer and the customers, she was finally sold to a merchant who needed a new kitchen slave and was willing to pay the regular price.

"She'll be better off than most," whispered Tirzah. "If she can cook well, they'll leave her alone. A master will show more mercy and patience with a good cook than with any other slave."

Deborah watched the fat man. She was relieved when she noticed that he did not seem to be doing any buying. Rather, he appeared to act as an adviser to other buyers, especially to a tall, well-dressed man with a lean, dignified face and graying hair.

Most of the slaves sold quickly except for the older men. Nobody wanted them. The mob jeered.

"Who do you think you are, Shamma, trying to palm those withered hides of asses off on us? Massa, you should have left their bones to bleach in the wilderness. This one here doesn't look as if he could do enough work in a day to earn food for a flea."

Shamma, the auctioneer, called an attendant, who brought some sacks of grain onto the platform. Jared and Eglon, the two slaves, were made to lift first the smallest and then the largest and heaviest sacks and carry them back and forth several times. Perspiration rolled from their faces, and their eyes bugged out with the strain.

"See for yourself! They can work," Shamma assured the farmer who had appeared interested in buying. After much beating down of the price, he led them away like two animals.

Deborah's heart sank. "Beasts of burden. That's all they are now. They won't live long if they have to work as hard as that. But if they hadn't shown they could carry loads, no one would have bought them, and they would have been killed right away," she thought, and shuddered.

It was now Ethan's turn. The gray-haired man motioned to the fat one, and together they examined the boy closely.

"What do you think, Obal?" asked the gray-haired man. "Nice muscles, eh? He has an intelligent face and might be teachable."

"Quite so, honorable Meshir." The fat man narrowed his little eyes and made a clicking sound with his tongue. "But the lad has rather a proud look and will take some taming. Not that it couldn't be done," he added quickly. "If you can buy him for——" He leaned over to whisper a price in the ear of his companion.

Meshir nodded. "We shall see."

The bidding for Ethan was much more brisk than for the

older slaves. A young army officer in a flounced tunic and a short brown cloak kept bidding against Meshir until the latter shrugged his shoulders as if to say, "Oh, well, you may have him if your heart is so set on it."

Ethan was sold to the captain for thirty-two pieces of silver. Shamma beamed. It was the highest price of the day so far.

"Good luck," whispered Deborah as Ethan's new master took him past her on their way out.

The boy nodded curtly to her. His eyes had lost some of the hard look that had worried her when they first met.

"Maybe we'll meet again," she thought. "Maybe Ethan will still become my good friend."

"And now we come to the final item up for sale," continued Shamma as he turned to Deborah and ordered her onto the platform.

Deborah felt as if her stomach were going in circles inside her. Her turn so soon? The last item? What about Tirzah? Her head whirled, and she flushed with nervousness when she stepped onto the display stage. Her ears rang, and a red haze blurred her eyesight.

From somewhere far away she heard the auctioneer saying, "And notice the fair skin, which is most unusual with the dark hair and eyes. A healthy-looking child with promise of great beauty. It is an advantage to buy a girl like this when she is young. She can be trained easily in fine manners and skills. She comes from a good home and should appeal to the most discriminating buyer. However, we have decided that the customer who wants to secure this very attractive slave must also be willing to take this other girl named Tirzah."

The mob snickered. The auctioneer raised his hand to call

for order. "Really, this is an unusual opportunity, for what Tirzah lacks in beauty, she makes up for in strength and willingness to work. Two valuable slaves to the same buyer! Who wants to examine the slaves?"

Deborah wanted to sink right through the wooden planks on which she was standing. "After that kind of talk Tirzah will hate me worse than ever. Oh, dear! And I thought she was beginning to feel a little more kindly toward me!"

As in a nightmare she watched the two men who had almost bought Ethan. She clinched her teeth and braced herself while the older man, Meshir, observed her closely. Obal was standing nearby, and Deborah hated his look even worse than that of Meshir, who might as well have been studying a peach or a melon to see if it was a good buy.

"Not bad at all," admitted Meshir in a whisper to Obal. "They may not be able to work hard to begin with, but later they'll be worth many times the price we pay today. Especially the younger one."

Obal agreed. "Honorable Meshir, it will be a profitable investment. I'll do my best to train them to your full satisfaction."

Meshir smiled. "You haven't failed me yet." Turning to Shamma, he said, "I'll start the bidding with five pieces of silver."

Deborah stared at the two men as though the sky had fallen. So Obal was the slave master for Meshir! If Meshir bought her and Tirzah, she dared not think of the kind of training they would receive at the hands of the fat man with the cruel face. If only someone else would outbid them!

But in the end no one did. When the price went above forty pieces of silver, the other buyers withdrew, and the two girls were sold to Meshir for forty-two silver coins.

Obal grinned and motioned for the girls to follow him. Deborah walked as in a trance. Her worst imaginings had come true. What was there left for her now? Had God forsaken her after all?

She heard the two men talking. Obal was saying, "Do you think the price was a bit steep?"

"Have no fear," Meshir replied. "Naaman has full confidence in my business sense, or he wouldn't have put me over all his affairs. Besides, it was at his command that the raiding party went out and brought the slaves here, so part of the price will come back to him. He'll have no reason to complain."

"Naaman!" thought Deborah. "The Syrian general who makes all Israel tremble! The man who is to blame for my capture! Meshir is the steward of Naaman's house, and now I'm Naaman's slave! I might as well be dead!"

4

In Naaman's House

Naaman's house was an impressive complex of buildings, large and small. Deborah, Tirzah, and their two masters entered from the street through a heavy gate guarded by a slave, who clanged it shut behind them. Deborah felt imprisoned already.

Obal clapped his hands, and an elderly female slave appeared. She was dressed in a long, loose tunic of coarse linen. Deborah noted with relief that she had a kind face.

Obal frowned. "Oh, it is you, Helah. Where is Eglah? Didn't she know I might bring some new slaves home today?"

"Yes, she was told, but Atarah wanted to see her about some matter. She hasn't returned from the house yet."

"Very well then, you may take these two to their quarters and give them something to eat. When Eglah is free, she can decide what work each one is best fitted for. Honorable Meshir, I shall report to you later."

Meshir consented with an absentminded wave of the hand.

The two girls followed Helah through the cobblestone courtyard, where many slaves worked at various tasks. The yard was as big as a marketplace, Deborah felt. It was enclosed on all sides with buildings and workshops. In one corner two brawny slaves sharpened swords in a blacksmith

36

shop. Next to them a slave tanned hides to be made into saddles, shoes, and other leather goods. Then followed a weaver's shop. This was a large room with many looms where girls made cloth to be used for the clothing of other slaves. There was a kitchen, a bakery, a room for trimming and filling oil lamps, and even a jewelry shop, where a slave of special skill painstakingly fitted together pieces of ivory, gold, and precious stones to make rare ornaments.

When Obal entered the compound, everybody stopped talking and bent more closely over his work.

Helah indicated to the girls the rawhide whip hanging on the wall of one of the rooms. "Obal knows how to use that," she whispered. "Don't ever displease him if you value your skin. Or Eglah either, for that matter." She looked around to make sure no one was listening. "You can never be too careful," she explained. "I've been here long enough to know that the walls have ears. Eglah always finds out what's going on. If a slave complains, she tells Obal. The two of them are just like this." She held up two fingers.

"Who is Eglah?" Deborah wanted to know.

"Bless you, you don't know much, do you? Eglah is the head of all the female slaves who work outside the house. You'd better get along with her if you know what's good for you. Here, this is where you sleep."

She led them into a dark corridor and pushed open a creaky door. In the dim light the girls could see a small room with no windows. There was no furniture, but piles of straw on the dirt floor were obviously intended to serve as beds.

Helah waved her hand in the direction of the rest of the corridor. "These are the quarters of the female slaves. We keep them clean ourselves. I'll take you back to the yard and show you where the slaves' kitchen is. Maybe you'll work there to begin with. We could use some more help. If you do your work well, Eglah may let you work in the garden or turn you over to Atarah to work in the kitchen in the big house."

"Well, now, who is putting ideas into the heads of these two newcomers?" said a sharp voice from a doorway nearby.

Deborah jumped.

"My, my, you are a skittish one!" continued the voice. Then a sharp-faced woman came into the light, and Deborah knew who it was even before Helah stammered, "I'm sorry, Eglah. I was just telling them how important it is to work faithfully if they ever hope to better themselves."

"Too bad you never learned to hold your tongue about things that don't concern you. You might have bettered yourself a little by now if you had."

Eglah surveyed her new charges with a critical look. Deborah stared back, fascinated as a bird might be with a snake about to devour it. Eglah was the thinnest woman she had ever seen. "She is so angular that you might get hurt if you bumped into her," Deborah thought. Two penetrating eyes peered out above a hawklike nose, eyes with no light of kindness like Helah's. Her mouth was slit above a pointed chin. Her hands were bony, like claws. She grabbed Deborah's arm with one of them and held it tight. Deborah swallowed hard and returned her gaze without flinching.

"Hm-m-m-m. You look like a sassy little one. Better watch your step with me! Good looks aren't everything, you know. Work is more important. You," she turned to Tirzah, who cowered in the shadow of the doorway, "you look as if you know how to behave. But no shirking on the job, and no whining! I'll put you both in the outside kitchen for a start. Take them there, Helah. I have more important things to do."

"Thank goodness for that," thought Deborah. "And thank goodness that Helah is kind, at least. If I can make friends with her and stay out of trouble with Eglah, things won't be all black. I may stay here for a long time and never even have to see Naaman."

One afternoon several months later Deborah was carrying a basket of vegetables through the courtyard. She was so anxious not to drop any of them that before she knew it she bumped into someone passing by. She looked up, frightened, but her face broke into a big smile when she recognized Ethan.

He smiled, too, and said, "Let me carry that. It's too heavy for a girl." He took the basket from her hands and walked with her to the kitchen. He sat on the courtyard pavement while she worked by the kitchen door, peeling onions and chatting happily.

"You look fine, Ethan," she said, stealing a glance at him out of the corner of her eye. "Your master must be kind."

"Yes, Captain Hadad is a good master," he admitted. "He feeds me well and insists that I wear clothes worthy of one who belongs to his household. The work isn't hard. I take care of his horses, polish his weapons, and see that his armor is always in order."

"An armor-bearer!" she gasped. "Captain Hadad must think a lot of you if he gave you a responsible position like that."

He smiled with satisfaction. "Yes, it seems that Baal is taking better care of me than your God is of you. Oh, I'll admit that the household of Naaman is an important place to serve, but here you are still just working in the slaves' kitchen."

She sighed. "Well, Eglah believes in a testing period where every girl has to prove her worth. This is not the nicest work, I know; but at least I get plenty to eat. And Helah is in charge of the cooking now. She's kind to me. I have a lot to be thankful for. But I forgot to ask what you're doing here, Ethan."

"My master had an appointment with Naaman. He told me to wait here. Have you ever seen the general, Deborah?"

"No. He doesn't come through the slaves' court. He leaves and enters by another gate. I don't want to see him. When I was a little girl in Israel, mothers used to make their children behave by threatening that Naaman would capture them."

"Do you still believe God will someday lead you back there?"

Deborah hesitated. "That depends on God. I know He is watching over me. And over you, too, Ethan, even though you think it is Baal who has prospered you. I've been praying to God for you every night. You should thank Him, not Baal, for your good fortune."

Ethan was speechless for a moment. The silence was broken by Tirzah, who came from the back of the kitchen, where she had been pounding meal for bread.

"So here she is, preaching again," she jeered. "I tell you, Ethan, this girl is so cheerful about everything that it makes me sick. Wait till she gets into some real trouble, and we'll see what she has to say about God watching over her."

Deborah pressed her lips together and said nothing. She had learned long ago that this was the most satisfactory reply to Tirzah's tirades.

"Come on, you two," called Helah. "It's time to eat. Deborah, after you carry this bowl of soup to Obal, you may serve the boy here. His master is dining with Naaman. Tirzah, you take this to Eglah before we serve the rest of the slaves. Be quick about it now!"

Tirzah was much faster than Deborah. She was already on her way back when Deborah approached Obal, gingerly carrying the bowl of hot soup.

No one knew exactly what happened, but Ethan could have sworn he saw Tirzah's foot shoot out just in time. Deborah, whose eyes were riveted on the bowl, tripped, and the scalding liquid hit Obal's left arm.

After the slave master's first bellowing cry of pain, a deadly silence settled on the courtyard. Deborah stood there thunderstruck, staring at the clay fragments of the bowl on the pavement and the ugly red blister on Obal's fat body. Eglah was the only one who kept her wits about her. She darted about, ordering terrified slave girls to bring cold water, ointments, and rags, while she kept up a stream of words violently scolding Deborah.

Under her expert treatment Obal recovered sufficiently to turn to the trembling girl. His face was as calm as ever and his voice under perfect control when he said, "I'm afraid you haven't learned, my child, that we do not tolerate clumsiness in a slave. We shall have to teach you a lesson, so that this will never occur again. We need to make an example of you. Jachin, Teron, bind her to the post, and bring me my lash!"

Two slaves seized Deborah, bared her back, and tied her to the whipping post in the center of the courtyard. She pressed her face against the wood, and her lips moved as if in prayer. She knew she might die under the lash as many slaves had done. But she also knew God could save her.

"Lord, You saved Joseph from death when he was falsely accused," she murmured. "Save me now if it is Your will."

Helah covered her eyes with her hands. Tirzah had a look of horrified triumph in her eyes as if to say, "Now we shall see if her God is watching over her." Ethan felt his blood boil in anger, both at Tirzah's trickery and his own helplessness.

Obal raised the lash. It cut through the air with a sickening swish. Deborah screamed out in pain. Blood trickled down from a long red welt on her skin. She closed her eyes and clenched her fists, trying not to cry again. But the second stroke was worse than the first, and again she screamed.

"What's going on down there? Obal, isn't that the slave we bought from Shamma; one of those that Massa brought from Israel?" All eyes turned to a balcony on the side of the big house facing the court. Meshir had stepped out and was surveying the scene with displeasure.

Obal let the lash sink slowly to the ground. "The same one, honorable Meshir. I'm giving this slave a much-needed lesson in carefulness and courtesy. May I proceed now?"

"One moment, Obal. I'll be right down."

An excited buzzing began among the slaves, but it was quickly silenced by Obal's fierce scowl. Deborah drew a deep breath. Eglah and Tirzah looked almost as puzzled and disappointed as Obal.

Presently Meshir made his way to the scene of torture. Although he was Obal's superior, he weighed his words carefully in the presence of all the other slaves. He studied the victim closely. "Hm-m-m, just as I thought. I don't question your judgment, Obal. Your methods of discipline have always worked in the past. But it so happens that when I bought this slave, I had some special plans for her. That was the reason I was willing to pay such a high price. I have been so busy that I must confess I had forgotten about this child until just now when I heard her cry. You may recall that one of the reasons I bought her was her beautiful face and complexion. Now, we simply cannot afford to mar her skin like this. We must find some other method of punishment. Or maybe we shall say that for this first offense she has been punished enough already. Obal, have Eglah take care of the child's wounds, and when they have healed, have her report to Atarah for training in duties inside the house."

When her tormentor ordered Deborah released, she crumpled in a heap on the ground.

"Fainted already, after only two stripes," muttered Eglah gruffly. "She deserved a lot more; that's what I say. But we must obey Meshir's orders. Here, carry her to her room. I'll send some girls to take care of her."

Obal's eyes glittered with hate. "Work in the house," he repeated to himself. "A promotion—after what she did to me! She'd better not cross me up again. I'll not be stopped next time."

Ethan turned to Helah. "I must find out how she is. Will you do me a favor? Deborah told me how kind you are. I can see that it's true. Please tell her I know her God must have been watching over her today. I'll wait here till you return."

"She's better now," Helah said when she came back. "She opened her eyes and smiled when I told her what you said. Then she asked me to tell you this: 'If you trust in God, even the worst will turn out to be for the best!' Now, wasn't that a strange thing for her to say?"

5

DEBORAH'S TEST

The next time Ethan saw Deborah, she had completely recovered from her ordeal. He had accompanied his master on another appointment with the general and was waiting for him in the outer hall of Naaman's house. Seated on the floor, as was proper for a slave, he was admiring the wall paintings running the entire length of the room. The rustle of a drapery and a faint giggle distracted him for a moment. There was Deborah, peering at him from a doorway. Her face was sunny and full of laughter.

"You have no idea how funny you look, sitting there as solemn as a judge," she said. "Do you like the paintings? They're supposed to describe all Naaman's victories in battle."

"Never mind the paintings! How are you? Are you getting along all right? You look awfully different from the last time I saw you."

Her face lost its merriment. "I know. It was terrible. I shall never forget it. But isn't it wonderful how the Lord turned it to good for me? If Meshir hadn't heard my cry, he might not have remembered me for a long time. Now I'm working for Atarah, head of the house slaves, and she is very kind. God has been good to me."

She smoothed her white linen tunic and straightened her red girdle, which gathered the tunic in at the waist. She was

44

taller and more slender than when they first met in the wilderness. Her hair, held in place by a red band circling her forehead, hung in shining waves around her radiant face.

Ethan nodded in spite of himself. "I must admit that it looks that way. It was a miracle the way Meshir came to your rescue at the right moment. It has been the talk of the slaves all through the city. But I bet Obal isn't too happy about the affair."

Deborah looked grave. "He will never forgive me. But I see very little of him, nor of Eglah. She doesn't like me either, but she can't harm me anymore. Atarah is different. She's patient with me when I make mistakes. I've learned how to dust the furniture and polish the floors. She's teaching me how to arrange flowers and wait on the table. I love to work in this beautiful house. It's cool and pleasant here. I wish Tirzah could work in here, too. This summer heat is making her sick. Every night when I go to the slave quarters to sleep, she complains about it. I've tried to get Atarah to find some work for her inside. Maybe she will soon."

Ethan stared at her with open mouth. "For Tirzah? After what she did to you that day you were whipped? I saw her trip you, you know. She did it on purpose to make trouble for you."

It was Deborah's turn to stare. "Are you sure, Ethan?" she whispered. "How could she do such a thing, even though she hates me?"

"I don't know. Why does she hate you so, Deborah? Did you mistreat her when she was your slave?"

"No, never. I ordered her about too much, I know. And once she got beaten for something that was my fault—but not with a whip, nothing like that," she hastened to add. "I think she hates me because we were about the same age;

I was happy and free and had a good father and mother, and she was sad because her own father had sold her as a slave. I never thought of it then; but since I came here, I've tried to understand it. If she would only believe in God, she would stop hating me. She couldn't hate anybody then. I won-der——"

"Deborah!" called a voice from down the long hall.

"I must run! Atarah wants me. I shouldn't be talking to you this long. Good-bye, Ethan. I'm glad I got to see you. As for Tirzah, I still think I may win her with kindness."

She disappeared behind the draperies and left Ethan with his own puzzled thoughts. He scratched his head. "What a strange girl! How could anyone win a girl like Tirzah with kindness? I hope Deborah leaves her alone. If they work together inside the house, nothing but trouble will come of it."

Deborah found Atarah in the garden court, a paved patio surrounded on three sides by part of the house and on the fourth by the garden itself. The head of the house slaves was a pleasant, plump Egyptian woman of graceful bearing. She was arranging a large bouquet of roses and lilies when Deborah arrived, a little out of breath from running down the long hallway.

"Here, child, sweep up the leaves and petals on the floor," she ordered. "Did you finish polishing the tables in the ban-quet room?"

"Yes, Atarah; and I dusted the floor also."

"Already? I thought you would need more time. Help me carry these flowers in there right now, and I'll see how well you did your work."

Finding the tables as well as the floor spotless, Atarah rewarded Deborah with a smile. When they were walking back to the garden court, she said, "You're the first slave I've had who can perform a task both quickly and well. Most girls dawdle and drag out their work as long as possible, as if they hated every moment of it. But you—I don't quite understand you! Many times you sing while you work. What do you find to be happy about in the life of a slave?"

Deborah laughed. "I wouldn't say that being a slave makes me happy. When I was first stolen away from my home, I thought I would never be happy again. But I've much to be thankful for, even though I am a slave. What's the use of feeling sad and downcast? That would only make matters worse."

"I agree. Now some people, like myself, who have been born in slavery may feel quite contented, since we have never known any other life. But I've noticed that most slaves who have been stolen and sold here are bitter and sullen and have to be forced to work. What makes you different?"

Deborah had picked up the broom and started to sweep. She stopped for a moment on the steps leading down into the garden. "If I am different, as you say, it is because I worship the only true God, the One who made heaven and earth and everything in them. He is a God full of mercy and kindness. My parents taught me that He will watch over everyone who prays to Him, no matter where he is. I know He's with me and helps me all the time."

"Where do you keep this God?" asked Atarah eagerly. "He sounds like a good God. Do you have a statue of Him in your quarters so that I might pray to Him sometime, too?"

"No, no, Atarah! I told you, my God is the only true God! He's not a statue. He lives up there." She pointed to the sky. "He can't be kept in a little room like the gods in the temples. He can be everywhere and see everything. I can pray to Him no matter where I am. I ask Him to help me with my work. I thank Him for making the beautiful flowers for us to enjoy. Most of all I thank Him for helping me on the day when Obal was beating me. And I thank Him for letting me come into the house and work here with you," she concluded as she went back to her sweeping.

Atarah looked thoughtful. "You mean to tell me your God knows everything you do and helps you, even with such little things?"

"That's what my mother always said. And I've found out for myself that it's true. He knows why I'm here even if I don't. My duty is to do my work the best I can and trust in Him. Then I can ask Him to bless me. Do you understand now why I can still be happy, even though I'm a slave?"

Atarah was bewildered. "It sounds strange, I must say. But it's beautiful, too. You must tell me more sometime. Right now I hear the tinkle of the bell that tells me the mistress herself wishes to see me."

When Atarah returned, she was worried.

"What did Naaman's wife have to say?" Deborah asked.

"The banquet for this evening has been canceled. All that work for nothing! Well, there's no harm in having the rooms cleaned. It seems that our lord Naaman is not recovering from his illness as quickly as we thought. The banquet tonight was supposed to be a celebration of his being well again. Now his wife tells me she's sending for the physicians."

"What's the matter with Naaman?" Deborah asked. She thought as she said it, "How things have changed! I can say that name without trembling and without hate."

"I heard that he had a boil of some kind," replied Atarah. "But it was supposed to have healed long ago. However, he hasn't been feeling well lately. I hope it's nothing serious. It worries me."

She turned to go back into the house and remembered something. "By the way, Deborah, I forgot to tell you we're getting a new girl to help us tomorrow. Eglah is sending in Tirzah, the girl who came with you from Israel. That will give you one more thing to be happy about."

Deborah stared for a while at the door through which Atarah had disappeared. Her feelings were all mixed up.

"I ought to be happy for Tirzah. I even wanted her to come in here and work with me," she reminded herself. "But that was before Ethan told me what she did to me that day. What if she tries to make trouble again? I can ask God to help me forgive her, but can I ever feel safe with her around?"

Tirzah's disposition did not improve with her new position. Deborah needed all the patience and self-control she could muster to keep sweet when Tirzah let loose with her acid tongue as they worked together. To make matters worse, Atarah became ill with a severe fever, and Eglah was brought in to supervise all the girls of the household. Deborah worked harder than ever, determined that Eglah should have no cause to find fault with her. She discovered that, for some reason, this only angered Eglah more. There was nothing the hawk-eyed supervisor detested as much as having to admit that a task of Deborah's had been performed perfectly.

"She still dislikes me for the mistake I made before," sighed Deborah one morning. "No matter what I do, Eglah will not change her mind about me. It seems hopeless!"

She was feeding the pet peacocks which roamed the lower garden. Noticing several of the colorful tail feathers on the ground, she picked them up and carried them to the house. They were prized as ornaments, and she had instructions to hand them over to Eglah whenever she found any.

As she walked through one of the rooms, a breeze blew in through the open window. It brushed the feathers against her nose, and before she knew it, she was seized with a violent spell of sneezing. She didn't notice until too late that she was walking too close to one of the tables. Her elbow bumped against a vase and sent it crashing to the floor.

Deborah thought her heart would stop beating. "Oh, dear, what have I done? One of the Egyptian vases Naaman prizes so highly as a war trophy! What will I do? He'll have me killed when he finds out!"

She looked around the room. She was alone. No one had seen what happened. Not stopping to think, she turned and fled back to the garden.

"Why should anyone find out?" she thought. "No one saw me! It was an accident. When Eglah discovers it, she won't know whom to blame. Certainly she won't blame me; she knows I've been working out here. If Atarah were in charge, I wouldn't be afraid to tell her. But Eglah—never!"

She took a deep breath to quiet her throbbing heart. Then she laid the feathers aside and began weeding the flower beds industriously as if nothing had happened.

It seemed only a few minutes later that she heard a noise from the house. She recognized Eglah's loud voice in a torrent of scolding, though she was too far away to make out her words. Then there were other voices, all talking at once, mingled with sobbing and the sound of running feet.

Deborah became uneasy. For a moment the commotion died down. She was beginning to breathe easier when suddenly the air was rent by a bloodcurdling scream from the courtyard. Deborah stood frozen in her tracks. Then she ran toward the yard to see what was happening.

There by the whipping post stood Tirzah. A slave was bringing Obal's lash, but even before she felt its murderous sting on her naked back, Tirzah was yelling and begging for mercy.

"What in the world is going on?" whispered Deborah to Helah, although she had a sickening feeling that she already knew.

"Oh, it's terrible," explained Helah hurriedly. "Eglah sent Tirzah into the Egyptian chamber a little while ago to dust and polish. When she came back to see how she was doing, there stood Tirzah, staring at a broken vase on the floor. And then she had the nerve to deny that she did it. They say all slaves lie, but can you imagine it? With the proof right there! Eglah is furious. I never liked Tirzah, but just the same this is a horrible way to die."

"There!" whispered a little voice inside Deborah. "This is your chance to get even with Tirzah. She's only getting what she should have had the last time when she made you taste the whip. Your life will be much easier when she's gone."

Another voice rang in Deborah's heart like a bell: "Thou shalt not bear false witness against thy neighbour."

How often she had heard her father say it and then add, "Sometimes, my children, silence at the wrong time can be the same as a false witness."

What would her father want her to do at a time like this? What would God want her to do?

What was it Joseph had said when he was tempted to do wrong: "How then can I do this great wickedness, and sin against God?"

Obviously there was only one right answer to Deborah's unspoken questions.

Her decision was swift and firm. She felt a great calm settle upon her as she stepped out of the crowd and called to Obal, "Tirzah is innocent. I broke the vase!"

6

A Mistress and a Maid

For the second time in Deborah's short stay in the house of Naaman, the bustling courtyard was as silent as a grave. No one spoke. No one hardly dared even breathe. Even Eglah was dumbfounded, and Obal stared at Deborah as if he had never seen her before.

She returned his look without flinching. "It is strange," she thought, "to have this peace in my heart when I know I shall die."

Obal still did not speak. He silently motioned for his attendants to release Tirzah. At this she started to sob again, this time in incredulous relief, and was led away to the house. The spell had been broken, and Obal turned to Deborah. He had found his usual evil smile.

"So at last I am privileged to settle a score with you," he purred. "You admitted your guilt, and this time Meshir is not here to save you. I'm in charge while he's on an errand for our master. Tie her to the post. This will give me great pleasure."

"Not so fast, Obal," came a voice from a latticed window in the upper story of the house.

The slave master looked up with an angry snarl on his lips. But when he realized who was talking, he bowed to the ground. "Mistress! It is you! I await your bidding."

53

"Send the child to me at once, Obal," commanded Naaman's wife. "I want to speak with her. A slave who will risk death to tell the truth interests me."

As though in a dream, Deborah walked into the house and to the upper story. Many a time she had helped carry water upstairs for her mistress's bath, or swept the halls, or watched from a respectful distance when Naaman's beautiful wife passed by. But only the most favored slave girls were allowed inside the apartments of the mistress.

"What does my mistress want?" she thought. "What will she do with me? She saved me from the lash, but will she send me back again after she has seen me?"

A door opened, and a girl motioned Deborah to enter. She was taken through one room after another, until she reached a room furnished with rich silk hangings and soft carpets. There were low couches and carved tables and cushions covered with damask, woven with threads of silver and gold. Large jars filled with flowers stood on the floor, and cages with singing birds hung from the ceiling.

But Deborah had eyes only for the slender woman in a blue and crimson robe, resting on a couch by the window. She bowed to the floor to Shelomith, the wife of Naaman.

"Arise, my child, and come over here where I can look at you," Shelomith said. Her voice was soft, and she was smiling. Shelomith was renowned in Damascus for her beauty. Some praised her large, luminous eyes; others claimed it was her perfectly formed features and exquisite coloring which distinguished her most. But what mattered to Deborah at that moment was the expression of kindness and gentleness which made her mistress's face radiant with a greater beauty. She knew now that this woman would not send her back to torture and death.

"Sit down here by me. That's much better. Atarah has told me about you. She said you are different from other slaves because you are cheerful and contented and enjoy doing your work well. But she didn't tell me you are also unusually truthful and very, very brave. That I have seen for myself today. You knew you might die; that you would be lashed to death if you stepped forward and told the truth about what had happened to the vase, didn't you?"

"Yes, Mistress."

"Then why did you do it? Tell me just what did happen before I heard Tirzah's cries and looked out."

It was easy to explain the whole unhappy incident to such a sympathetic listener. Before she knew it, Deborah had poured out the story of the broken vase.

"So you see, Mistress, I was not brave at all when I ran away to the garden instead of telling Eglah! I'm ashamed of that part. But I never thought she would blame someone else. And then, Tirzah of all people."

Shelomith nodded thoughtfully. "Knowing Eglah, I can easily understand why you acted that way. But you were brave when it really counted, my dear. Braver than any girl I have ever seen. But what do you mean by 'Tirzah of all people'? Is she a special friend of yours? I was told she came from Israel with you."

"Not a friend exactly, Mistress, although I have tried to make her my friend," Deborah said.

Shelomith sensed a story behind the story. "Come on, come on; tell me all about you and Tirzah," she urged.

This pretty child with the shining eyes fascinated her. Not for a long time had she had such diversion. She settled back while Deborah recounted the history of her capture and the events since then, trying to put Tirzah in as favorable a light as possible. This was not an easy task. Shelomith, with her knowledge of the ways of slaves, read much of the truth between the lines. As the real meaning of Deborah's act dawned on her, Shelomith's eyes filled with tears.

"You were willing to die," she whispered, and took Deborah's hand in hers; "you were willing to take that horrible punishment for a girl who has been so unkind to you! No, I know you didn't say it in so many words! But I hear things, too, you see. I know a great deal more about what goes on than you think. How could you do it? Most girls, and men, too, would have said nothing."

"Saying nothing right then would have been the same as telling a lie, Mistress. My parents taught me the law of God, and it says, 'Thou shalt not bear false witness against thy neighbour.' I couldn't let someone else be punished for my mistake."

"And you would rather die than disobey your God? Does your God always ask that of you? It seems a hard thing." Shelomith looked searchingly at Deborah.

"No, He doesn't always ask it, Mistress. Most of the time His laws are not hard to obey. But if obeying His will should bring death, then that is better than to disobey Him and live to feel guilty and ashamed."

"You have not only courage and honesty; you also have wisdom far beyond your years. Deborah, I've decided you are the girl I have been looking for. I want you to stay here with me and be my personal maid. I shall send word to Eglah at once."

She reached for a silver bell on the table by her side. At its tinkle a servant girl appeared and was given the message. She bowed and left.

Shelomith turned to the speechless Deborah. "Now,

there, at last you are smiling," she said. "Are you happy now?"

"Happier than I have been since the day I first came to Syria! I shall serve you faithfully as long as you need me. And may the Lord God of heaven bless you for your kindness to me," stammered Deborah.

Shelomith's own smile faded. "I wish I could believe that your God would bless me," she said. "Slaves are not the only people who have troubles, Deborah. I'm tired, child. Let Rana show you to your room and tell you about your duties. I shall see you in the morning."

During the days that followed, Deborah learned to feel not only gratitude, but love toward her mistress. Her tasks were easy and pleasant, and she had complete freedom of the house and the gardens. At last Naaman's wife had found one person whom she felt she could trust completely, and often she called Deborah to her room to talk to her.

Shelomith was especially interested in learning more about Deborah's faith in God. This was a request the girl was only too happy to fulfill.

"My cup is full of joy," said Deborah to Atarah on the day Atarah was well enough to return to her duties. "Even Tirzah has changed toward me at last. After what happened, she doesn't distrust me anymore. She doesn't even appear to be jealous of my new position. Now, if our lord Naaman could only get well, so that my lovely mistress would be happy again. It hurts me to see the sadness in her eyes every time she visits him. I wish I could do something to help her!"

"You have helped her already, child," Atarah assured her. "She enjoys having you around. She's taken a new interest in the affairs of the household. What happened to you has made her understand things she never realized before about Eglah and Obal and the way they treat the other slaves. Believe me, the household is breathing easier because of you. You said once that your God knew why you were sent here as a slave. Well, do you know what I think? You came here because we needed relief from Obal's cruelty—that's why! Mistress Shelomith has laid down the law to him."

"I'm glad you think I've helped. But there is so much more I would like to do. If I only knew how to go about it! Oh, there's the bell. I must run, Atarah."

She raced up the stairs and into Shelomith's rooms.

Rana met her with a finger laid to her lips. "Sh-h-h, child, not so lively. Our mistress is not feeling well. She's resting, but she wishes to see you. Go in quietly. Do not speak until she speaks to you."

On tiptoe Deborah approached the inner chamber. She drew the curtain aside softly and paused on the threshold. Shelomith was lying on the couch with her face hidden in the pillows.

"She's asleep," thought Deborah. "I'll get the ointments and perfumes ready so that she can have her bath when she awakes." She moved quietly through the room toward the side chamber, where she could work without disturbing her mistress.

But Shelomith was not asleep. She lifted her head and called, "Is that you, Deborah?" Her voice had the sound of utter despair, and one look at her flushed, tear-stained face brought Deborah quickly to her side.

"Mistress! Oh, Mistress, what has happened? Are you ill? Shall I have Rana call the physicians? Let me bring some water to bathe your face."

Shelomith shook her head wearily. "Never mind! Come

and sit here with me. The physicians just left. They've been with my husband all afternoon. Oh, Deborah, it's terrible!" She began to tremble. "They say—they say Naaman will never get well. He has leprosy! That means he will suffer horribly, and die. My husband is a leper!"

7

"Naaman Is a Leper"

"Naaman is a leper!"

Shelomith's words left Deborah stunned. When her mistress started to sob violently again, she could think of nothing to do but sit there and pat her shoulder. Seeing Shelomith's grief brought the tears to her own eyes, and she wept in quiet sympathy. "What will happen now? If this were Israel, Naaman would be forced to leave his home and live alone in some desolate place. What will my poor mistress do?"

Finally Naaman's wife stopped her sobbing and lay exhausted on her couch. The sight of Deborah's tears brought her an unexpected sense of comfort.

"You dear child," she whispered. "Many times these past few months, when I was worried about my husband's health, your smiles and your joyfulness brought me cheer. Now when the worst has happened, you weep with me, and that, too, soothes my grief a little. How strange that you, a maid of Israel, should cry over the misfortune of Naaman, the general who has defeated the armies of your land and whose soldiers stole you to be a slave."

"Mistress, I cry because you are sad, and because I love you. And even though I was taught to think of Naaman as an enemy, I know he must be a good man, or you wouldn't love him so much. But what will happen now?"

"I don't know, Deborah. My husband must have had this illness longer than we think, maybe even since his last military campaign. The physicians thought he was troubled with boils. Now when all their treatments have brought no healing, they're sure it's leprosy. Naaman is sending word to the king, asking Benhadad himself to decide what ought to be done."

"Is the—the sickness very bad yet?" Deborah dared to ask. She shuddered when she thought of the lepers she had seen in Israel, with fingers or toes rotted away, or with an ugly cavity where the nose or an ear should have been. There would be beggars like that outside the city gate at home, crying, "Unclean! Unclean!" and hoping someone would take pity and throw them a crust of bread.

"No, it has been progressing very slowly. That's why the physicians have not been sure. But it's getting worse. And, Deborah, they admit they have no cure. It's a living death. I feel I want to die, too."

"Mistress, let me bring scented water and bathe your face. It will make you feel better," Deborah insisted. "You must be able to receive the messengers when they return with word from the king. All hope is not lost yet."

"You are right, child. Maybe Benhadad will think of something. He values my husband's services highly and has told him many times he has never had a better general. King Benhadad will do anything in his power to help us."

Shelomith sat up and allowed Deborah to bring the basins of water and the fragrant oils and creams. Rana was summoned after the bath to apply the usual cosmetics to her mistress's face. While Deborah held the polished bronze hand mirror, the older slave painted Shelomith's cheeks and lips and laid on the eye shadow a little heavier than usual to cover the swelling caused by her crying. Then the two girls dressed their mistress in her best robe of white silk, girdled and fringed with gold. They placed a gold band around her long, dark hair and hung gold chains around her neck and wrists.

"You look beautiful, Mistress," Deborah murmured, "beautiful and brave."

"Not as brave as I would like to be," answered Shelomith. "But as the wife of a brave man I think it is only fitting that I show the king's messengers courage in the face of disaster. I think I hear them coming through the courtyard. Deborah, tell Meshir I will receive them in the large hall."

A few minutes later the messengers from Benhadad bowed low before the gracious lady as she sat, sad-faced but erect, in a large carved chair on the dais in Naaman's audience chamber. This was the first time she had taken her husband's place in the seat of authority. It was a silent admission that from now on all his communications with the outside world would have to be carried on through others.

Deborah, on her way back upstairs after taking Shelomith's message to Meshir, let her curiosity get the better of her good manners and judgment. She crept close to the hangings by the door of the chamber and peered through a crack. Straining her eyes and ears, she saw the messenger undo a papyrus scroll and heard him begin to read:

"Benhadad, King of Syria, to Naaman, captain of the king's host, greetings!"

Just then Atarah's strong arms yanked her away, and Atarah's usually mild voice whispered sternly, "Up with you, where you belong! Slaves are not allowed here! You ought to be ashamed of yourself. If the mistress wants you to know what's in the message, she'll tell you. Now go!"

Deborah hung her head. She knew Atarah was right, and she hurried back to her duties. She worked with nervous haste, helping Rana tidy up the rooms, gather fresh flowers, and prepare a tray of fruit, cakes, and wine for the refreshment of their mistress when she returned. "Would Shelomith never come?" thought Deborah. Every moment seemed like an hour. "What would the king say? Would Naaman be banished from the court and from his home? What would become of his household and his many slaves?"

When the draperies finally were pulled aside and Shelomith appeared, it was easy to tell by the lightness of her step that the king's message had been favorable.

"Rana! Deborah! His majesty Benhadad is most gracious! He declares that he cannot do without Naaman's services as his chief general. He says that as long as my husband is able, he wants him to remain here in Damascus, and with his wise counsel and his battle experience he can still be the leader of the Syrian armies. He will have to stay in his rooms, of course, but the king will continue to seek his counsel on all military matters. Furthermore, King Benhadad has announced a feast at which he himself will offer sacrifices and prayers to our great god Rimmon for my husband's healing. Surely Rimmon will be pleased to grant this favor to one who has honored him and Syria so nobly and brought great treasures of war to enrich his temple. You were right, Deborah; there is still hope—even for a leper!"

Deborah found an excuse to busy herself. She didn't feel like dampening her mistress's enthusiasm right then. But deep in her own heart she knew a god such as Rimmon could offer nothing but the bitterest disappointment to Naaman and his lovely wife.

The feast at Rimmon's temple was over. The sacrifices

had been offered. The incense had risen. The priests had chanted their magic incantations and studied the omens found in the livers of fowl and sheep. The physicians had moved their hands back and forth over Naaman's bowed head and murmured their secret formulas of healing. But there was no change in the general's condition. If anything, he was growing rapidly worse. A deep gloom settled over Shelomith, completely obscuring the hope she had felt at the message from the king.

Deborah's heart ached for her beloved mistress. She longed to help in some way. A daring idea had formed in her mind, but she was not sure Shelomith would listen to it. Since her disappointment at Rimmon's feast, Shelomith did not wish to talk to anyone about her husband's illness, but would sit by the hour staring out the window with eyes that saw nothing.

Still, the more Deborah thought about her idea, the more she knew she must talk to Naaman's wife.

One morning while she and Rana were arranging Shelomith's hair, she burst out, "Would God my lord were with the prophet that is in Samaria! for he would recover him of his leprosy."

The mirror fell from Rana's trembling fingers and clattered to the floor. The ivory comb fell on the rug as Shelomith turned quickly to face Deborah and ask, "Child, do you know what you are saying? Samaria is the capital of your country, our age-old enemy! You would suggest that my husband go there for healing? Are you out of your mind?"

"No, Mistress. I know the prophet Elisha could heal my lord Naaman. He has healed others. He is really your only hope!"

"Hope! Why talk about hope?" said Shelomith bitterly.

"Our own gods have not heard our prayers. Why should we seek help from the God of our enemies? Your God wouldn't heal Naaman, who has defeated your armies in battle. Besides, our gods are stronger than your Jahve, or we wouldn't have won over you. Deborah, I should be very angry with you for saying such a thing to me. But I know how you feel about your God. I agree He has blessed you and helped you. But would He do that for Naaman? Of course not!"

"Mistress, pardon me for contradicting you, but my God will help Naaman if you ask Him. My God is not only the God of Israel, He is the God of the whole world. He made the earth and everything in it. He permitted your king and your husband to defeat Israel to punish our people for worshiping false gods. That's what my father told me. Please, Mistress, listen to me! The gods of Syria have not helped our lord Naaman. They are only images of wood and stone. They have no ears to hear your prayers nor eyes to see your need. But my God can hear you, and His prophet can heal the sick." She stopped, suddenly aghast at her own boldness.

Rana stared at her, horror-stricken. A slave girl talking like this about the gods of her masters! Surely Rimmon would loosen one of his bolts of lightning and strike this impudent child dead on the spot!

But Shelomith was listening with a new light in her eyes. "We've tried everything, and it has failed," she admitted. "What is there to lose? I know your God is powerful, for I have seen how He has made you strong and brave and good. Your God must be pleased with you because you obey Him, so He may choose to hear your prayers. But this prophet about whom you speak? Can he heal even a leper?"

"I'm sure God will give the prophet power to heal our lord Naaman," Deborah answered eagerly. "The prophet

Elisha has performed many miracles. He even restored a dead boy to life. Isn't that greater than healing a leper?"

"If this prophet can heal my husband, Deborah, dear, both he and I will be as the dead who are restored to life. I must speak to Naaman at once! There's no time to lose."

Naaman gazed at his beautiful wife through the lattice which separated them. He hadn't seen her so full of hope since the day he last enjoyed good health. Now he was carefully weighing the suggestion she brought. "You say this girl has always told you the truth, Shelomith?"

"Yes, my dear, she is the one I told you about before, who would rather die than tell a falsehood."

"And what makes you so sure she's not setting a trap for me? After all, my soldiers took her away from her parents and brought her into slavery. If I go to Samaria to see this prophet, the Israelites might capture me or kill me. Then she would have revenge. Even if they let me return to Syria, but without being healed, it will be with shame on my head."

"Naaman, Deborah is devoted to me! Revenge is the farthest from her thoughts. I told you this child is different from any girl I've ever known, slave or free. She believes in her God so strongly that she's making me believe also. Besides, we're at peace with Israel now. They would not dare do anything that might start another war. Naaman, ask the king's permission to seek healing from this prophet. Please, my beloved! It's our only chance."

Naaman looked at the tears in Shelomith's pleading eyes. Then he glanced down at his hands, wrapped in bandages to hide the ugly leprosy that was eating away his fingers. He nodded. "I'll send word to the king. I'll do anything, even go to Israel, if I have a chance to get well again!"

8

Expedition to Samaria

"Deborah! Deborah! I must talk to you!"

Deborah almost dropped the roses she was picking in the garden to put in the rooms of her mistress. In the doorway leading to the long corridor and the great hall stood Ethan, grinning from ear to ear as if he were bursting with important news.

"Ethan! What are you doing here? Does your master know?"

"Don't fret yourself. My master is in counsel with Naaman about the journey to Israel. He gave me permission to seek you here when Atarah told us where you were. You've become an important person in Damascus, Deborah. Everybody's talking about the maid from Israel, and how on your word King Benhadad is sending an expedition to King Joram."

"Oh, that's not really of my doing, Ethan. The Lord has impressed Benhadad to do this. The king needs Naaman and will do anything to see him healed. Won't it be wonderful when Naaman returns home well and strong again?"

"You really believe he will, don't you? Well, he may or he may not. But I came to tell you something even more exciting. I'm going along, too!"

"Ethan! You're going to Israel!" In her cry there was a

67

mingling of joyous surprise and unspoken yearnings. Israel! She felt a lump rising in her throat as she pictured the snows of Mount Hermon and the hills of Gilead in their spring cloak of green. There in the valley she could imagine the city of Jabesh, and down a certain narrow alley a house with a flat roof and a large courtyard——

She blinked back the tears that stung her eyelids with hot persistence. "I'm so happy for you, Ethan," she managed to say in almost her natural voice. "Captain Hadad must have great confidence in you."

The boy's grin faded. "Yes, he needs me as his armor-bearer and private servant. Lucky for me Naaman picked him to command the soldiers that will be his escort. Don't you see what this means?" He glanced all about him and lowered his voice to whisper, "Once I'm in Samaria, I'll be free again. No more slavery for me!"

"Ethan, you wouldn't!"

"Run away? Oh, wouldn't I! Come on, Deborah; I don't like that offended look on your face. You don't believe I would go all the way home and then return here again as a slave when I'll have a hundred chances to escape? No, this is good-bye, Deborah. We leave tomorrow morning. I'm sorry you can't escape, too. You really deserve it. I'm trusting you not to tell anyone."

"Like Captain Hadad is trusting you not to run away?" she shot back at him. "Don't worry; I'm no bearer of tales. But you ought to be ashamed of yourself. Here Naaman and all this company are going to Israel because they believe our God is mighty to heal and to help. What will they think of our God and our people when you, an Israelite, cannot keep your word to your master, who has been so kind to you? I thought you had some pride!"

"I do! I'm too proud to remain a slave when I can be free." He lifted his chin and defied her with his eyes.

"It's better to be an honest slave, worthy of your master's trust, than to be a free man and a betrayer of his confidence," she warned him. "And God cannot bless you when you do wrong."

"Your God is not my god, Deborah," he said, irritated. "There are so many gods—how do I know which one to worship?"

She looked at him searchingly. After all she had told him about Joseph and Moses and Joshua and David, he still didn't believe! She sighed unhappily.

"Ethan, I wish you would promise me one thing. Stay with your master until Naaman has been healed by the prophet. Then decide which God is worthy of your worship. Will you do it?"

"I don't know. I don't want to make you a promise like that. It may be too hard to keep. Good-bye, Deborah! You—you have been a good friend. I hope for your sake the prophet can heal Naaman, for if he doesn't, it'll be too bad for you."

Deborah looked for a long time at the door through which Ethan had disappeared. Then she ran to the bottom of the garden and climbed up on her favorite corner of the wall. From here she could see the snowcapped towers of Mount Hermon, the same mountain whose foothills extended into the borders of Israel. On clear days its white summit could be glimpsed from heights near her own hometown.

Many thoughts whirled around in her mind. "I wonder how everything is with father and mother and Joel and Ira. Oh, I wish I could go along with the caravan tomorrow and see my family again! Do they still remember me? Do they think I'm dead? If only——"

She jumped down from her perch and ran to the house. She must see her mistress at once. Why didn't she think of this before?

The great hall in Naaman's house was bustling with activity. Shelomith sat on the dais, overseeing the work of Atarah and Rana. They in turn directed other women in preparing ten changes of raiment of the highest quality. These Naaman intended to give to the prophet Elisha as a reward for his services. Under Meshir's supervision trusted slaves were bringing bars of precious metal from Naaman's treasure chamber to be wrapped in sacks and carried on camels through the desert. Out in the courtyard the camels were being made ready for their heavy load of ten talents of silver and six thousand pieces of gold, intended as a gift for the prophet. A strong company of soldiers would be going along to guard the valuables and serve as the general's escort. Food, water, and other provisions were being packed. Nothing must be overlooked in order that the expedition would be a complete success.

Shelomith saw the excitement on Deborah's face when the girl entered the great hall and made her way through the busy crowd. She called her over. "Look, dear child, at what is happening here, and all because of you! Everyone is working. Everyone is eager. This house is no longer a place of gloom and despair. It's a place of hope."

"I'm glad. May God grant that soon it will be a house of joy and praise. Mistress, your kind words have made me bold. I have a special favor to ask of you."

Shelomith extended her hand as a token of blessing. Deborah knelt and kissed it.

"What is your request? Surely you've earned the right to make one. If it is within my power, I shall be glad to grant it."

Deborah's lovely face was pale and almost frightened as she formed the words with trembling lips, "The caravan of our lord Naaman will pass through the borders of Gad on its way to Samaria. Mistress, my parents do not know whether I am dead or alive. All this long time they've heard nothing from me. Do you think my lord Naaman might be willing to send a messenger to Jabesh-gilead to the house of Heber and tell him that his daughter is well?"

Shelomith felt a lump of compassion rising in her own throat when she saw the tears in her slave girl's eyes. She stroked Deborah's dark curls kindly. "Rise, my dear. I shall speak to my husband for you. If it is at all possible, the rider will be sent, and your parents shall receive good news of you."

Dismissing the overjoyed girl with a wave of the hand, she continued, "Now run back to your duties. We must all do our part so that the expedition can leave tomorrow at dawn. This is a great day in the house of Naaman!"

Even before the journey started, Ethan had decided that Samaria would be the best place for his attempt to escape. The caravan made its way across the border of Israel and through the mountain pass north of the waters of Merom, and his heart leaped at the sight of the hills and valleys of his homeland. He watched with mingled feelings when the promised messenger left for Jabesh-gilead and then later caught up with the slow-moving caravan to report his mission accomplished, a report that there was rejoicing in the house of Heber.

"I have no one who cares whether I'm alive or dead," thought the boy bitterly. "The pestilence took my mother, the Syrians killed my father, and my brother died under the curse of the prophet Elisha! And here I am a part of an expedition to see that same prophet and ask healing for a Syrian general! It makes no sense at all! But when I have escaped, everything will make sense at last!"

He tried to persuade himself that his plan was a just one and pushed far down deep in his mind the memory of Deborah's words and her accusing eyes as she had told him good-bye in Naaman's garden.

On the day when the towers of Samaria were sighted, Ethan's excitement grew to fever pitch. The plain of Shechem between Mount Ebal and Mount Gerizim had never looked so fair. Peasants were harvesting their early barley from the golden fields. They stopped swinging their sickles to gaze in undisguised amazement at the horse-drawn chariot carrying Naaman and at his retinue of cavalrymen, camels, servants, and foot soldiers. Ethan found himself straightening his back and looking ahead proudly as he carried his master's shield beside his slow, plodding horse, weary from the journey.

"I wonder if I'll see anyone I know in Samaria," he thought. "If Harim, the silver merchant, is still there, he will surely hide me when I run away. My father traded with him for years. I must plan everything carefully. I can't afford to make any mistakes."

The caravan halted on the outskirts of Samaria. Naaman and his leading officers, Hadad and Hazael, wanted to rest and refresh themselves and change their dusty garments before appearing before Joram, king of Israel, with the letter Benhadad had sent.

Ethan was carrying water to the camels from the nearby well when he noticed a tall, thin man walking slowly by. His sharp eyes were studying the caravan with a great deal of interest.

Ethan stared at the stranger. Or was he really a stranger?

Putting down the waterpot, he broke into a run. "Say, aren't you Gehazi, who used to be at Bethel some years ago? You used to live in the house under the big fig tree! Remember me, Ethan, son of Uriah?"

"Ethan! I would never have known you! You've grown up. Where have you been? What are you doing in this Syrian caravan?"

Quickly Ethan told him his story and his present mission. Gehazi's lean face grew thoughtful. He rubbed his bearded chin with his hand.

"Very interesting! So King Benhadad has sent a letter to King Joram, asking him to heal Naaman of his leprosy! Hm-m-m—wait till my master hears about this!" He turned and started for the city with long, loping strides.

"Wait a minute! Do you know whether Harim, the silver merchant, is still keeping his shop by the water tower?" Ethan asked anxiously.

"Sorry, my boy. Harim died only two months ago."

With that disappointing bit of news for Ethan, Gehazi was gone.

Ethan sighed and picked up his waterpot. He got back to the caravan just in time to be on call when the expedition started to move again, into the city and finally to the king's palace.

King Joram sat on his throne in the most impressive room in his palace, the "ivory house" built by his father, Ahab. All around the cedar wall paneling ran ornate borders of carved ivory inlays, with patterns of flowers, scrolls, strange-looking figures, and winged animals with human faces. The ivory lions adorning the king's chair had inset eyes of precious stones; and their open mouths were colored red, giving them a natural, ferocious appearance. But they looked no more fierce than the young king himself as he read for the second time the scroll containing the letter from Benhadad, king of Syria. It ended with these words: "Now when this letter is come unto thee, behold, I have therewith sent Naaman my servant to thee, that thou mayest recover him of his leprosy."

King Joram knit his brows in anger and suspicion as he let the scroll fall into his lap. He surveyed the group before him. There stood Naaman, at a respectful distance from everyone else. Once a greatly feared enemy of Israel, now he was laid low by the most dread disease of all. There were the officers and messengers of the king of Syria, awaiting his word as the ambassadors of Israel so often had been forced to do in the court of Benhadad when they had been sent there to sue for peace after defeat.

"There is a dangerous plot here," thought Joram. "Benhadad knows that no man, not even a king, can heal another man of leprosy. Benhadad is clever, and he is seeking a cause to wage war against me. But he is not going to trap me. I'll have nothing to do with this matter."

The king motioned for his counselors to come close. He conferred with them in whispers. The silence in the room grew oppressive. Naaman stood there tense. What was the king waiting for?

Dropping the scroll to the floor, Joram sprang to his feet. Grasping his robe of royal purple with both hands and pulling with all his might, he tore his garment in two with a ripping sound that sent terror to every heart. It was the sound of despair, of grief, and of defiance. To Naaman, it was the sound of hopelessness when he heard the king shout, with a face almost as purple as his robe:

"Am I God, to kill and to make alive, that this man doth send unto me to recover a man of his leprosy? Wherefore consider, I pray you, and see how he seeketh a quarrel against me. Benhadad desireth a cause to make war, that he may slay me as my father was slain by his men in the battle of Ramoth-gilead."

This was the end of Naaman's quest. The days and nights of hoping and longing, the weeks of tiresome traveling to seek help from the God of Israel, had ended in the throne room of Israel's king. Here was a man who knew less about the power of God than a humble slave girl, stolen from one of his border provinces.

Naaman bowed stiffly and motioned his retinue to leave with him. Silently the servants of Joram ushered them out. The watching crowd sensed danger in the air.

"We haven't heard the end of this matter," whispered one of Joram's retainers to a companion in the courtyard. Ethan, who had been told to wait outside, overheard and wondered what they meant. He knew from the expression on the faces of Naaman, Hadad, and Hazael that something had gone terribly wrong.

"Here, lad," Hadad said in a tone of barely controlled anger, "carry my things to the inn by the northern gate. We shall rest there tonight. Tomorrow we return to Damascus."

"Tomorrow!" Ethan felt as if he had been pierced by the very sword he was carrying. "That means I must escape tonight. My master is upset about something. He will not be keeping a sharp eye on me. If I could only find Gehazi again. He is the only one I know here. Maybe he would help me hide until the Syrians are tired of looking for me. I must act quickly. Tonight or never!"

9

A Message From the Prophet

The distinguished Syrian guests had eaten their evening meal at the inn by the north gate. Ethan had watered and fed his master's horse, groomed it, and rubbed it down. He had polished Captain Hadad's sword and shield to perfection and checked every arrow in the quiver. Now twilight was turning to darkness. He knew he must carry out his plan to escape as soon as possible while people were still coming and going through the gate of the inn. The watchman would not be so likely to notice a boy slipping out.

As he darted across the busy courtyard, he heard a voice shouting his name. He gave an involuntary start, but turned around slowly, pretending not to be nervous.

It was Donai, Naaman's personal physician, who had accompanied his master on the journey.

"Here, boy, you know this city, don't you?"

Ethan nodded. "What do you want?"

Donai slipped a coin into Ethan's hand. "Do you think you might find a perfumer's booth still open in the bazaar? Our lord Naaman requires some more of this ointment." From the folds of his girdle he produced a small jar, nearly empty. "Show this to the seller of balms, and he'll know what it is. Your master, Captain Hadad, was not too eager to give his consent to this errand, so make haste, boy!"

Ethan chuckled to himself as he slipped through the gate of the inn and scurried down the street, in the opposite direction from the bazaars. A feeling of wild elation gave wings to his feet.

"I never thought it would be so easy. The omens must be good for me tonight. First I'll see if the city gate is still open. If I can get out into open country, I can run to the hills while it's dark and hide in a cave during the day. This money will buy food for many days. My master will stop looking for me and go back to Syria. He might even think I was robbed and killed. I hope he notices that I did my work especially well tonight."

Thus Ethan mused to himself, trying to quiet his conscience while his flying feet took him farther and farther away from the inn and from the bazaars.

But when he got to the city gate, it was closed and barred, as was the custom at sunset. Ethan turned quickly away, not wanting to attract attention, as anyone would who lingered near the gate that late in the evening.

"I must hide somewhere in the city," he thought. "But where? If I could only find Gehazi!"

Turning a corner a little too swiftly, Ethan bumped right into two men who were coming toward him in a great hurry. He begged their pardon and was about to hurry on his way when one of them grabbed him and held him. Ethan looked up, terrified, then relieved. The lamplight from a nearby open door fell on the face of Gehazi.

"Gehazi!" he gasped, afraid to believe his good fortune. "I've been looking for you. Can you——"

"Looking for me? That's strange indeed. I've been looking for you. By the way, what are you doing here by the gate? Not running away, I hope!"

Ethan recognized a tone of suspicion in his voice and detected a strange, sly look in his narrow eyes. He decided against taking this man into his confidence for the time being. Instead, he pulled the jar of ointment out of his cloak and explained his errand.

"I thought you knew better than to look for the shop of the balm maker in this part of the city," said Gehazi. "I'll show you the way, and then you must take me to your master. This man with me is Heman, an officer of King Joram. He has an important message for Naaman, and so have I. The prophet Elisha sends word for Naaman to come and see him. King Joram cannot heal Naaman of his leprosy, but Elisha knows the Lord is able to give healing."

Ethan felt his head spinning. What was this all about? He had heard the other servants talking at the inn about what had happened at the palace, but he hadn't cared much whether Naaman was healed or not. He had thought only of his own escape. Now the whole situation was changed again, and Gehazi, the man he had known long ago in Bethel, was mixed up in this whole matter somehow. What a strange situation!

"It's odd," Ethan thought. "I was looking for Gehazi to ask him to help me escape. Now, of all people, he's the one who's taking me back to my master. He suspects me, but thanks to Donai and his errand, no one can prove I was running away. But what is Gehazi doing here? Does he work for the king, too?"

Aloud he said, "Gehazi, are you also an officer of King Joram, like Heman? You must have advanced very fast since I knew you."

Gehazi looked surprised. "Didn't you know that I'm the personal servant and helper of the prophet Elisha? It was fortunate I met you this morning so that I could tell my master about Naaman's arrival. Naturally it would be too bad to let such an important visitor return home without finding what he came for. Naaman's goodwill means much to the peace and understanding between our two countries."

A hard glint came into Gehazi's eye. "You also told me yourself that the general is bringing a rich reward. What a blessing that would be to my master's work, especially in helping the schools of the prophets," he concluded in a pious tone.

Ethan chided himself for his talkativeness earlier in the day. He was not so sure that he liked Gehazi at all. The way the fellow's eyes lighted up when he talked about the reward gave Ethan the feeling that not all of Naaman's silver and gold would find its way to the schools of the prophets.

He shrugged his shoulders when they reached the inn. "It is fate," he said to himself. "There's bound to be another chance for freedom. Next time I won't fail."

The king's officer and Gehazi bowed low to Naaman and his officers when they were ushered into their presence. Heman, the royal messenger, explained that King Joram sent his greetings and wanted the Syrian visitors to know that his action earlier was based on a misunderstanding. Then Gehazi was permitted to read the prophet Elisha's message to Joram concerning Naaman:

"Wherefore hast thou rent thy clothes? let him come now to me, and he shall know that there is a prophet in Israel."

Naaman looked up from the couch on which he was resting. He was weary with pain, travel, and worry, and weighed down by anger and disappointment. Now this message struck a note of hope. This sounded like the way the maid Deborah used to talk to Shelomith. He motioned to Donai to help him sit up.

"Worthy Heman, take my thanks to King Joram for his greetings. And you, Gehazi, tell your master, the prophet, that I shall seek his presence tomorrow before the third hour of the day. Now you may leave and God speed your going." Naaman sank back on the pillows. "Tomorrow!" whispered a voice in his heart. "I shall be healed tomorrow!"

At the appointed time the next morning the Syrian expedition halted outside a simple stone dwelling on the outskirts of Samaria. This was the house described to them the night before as the residence of the prophet Elisha.

"It certainly doesn't look like the home of an important man," muttered Ethan, half to himself and half to Donai, who was nearby. "If he has healed as many people as they say and collected rewards for his miracles, I wonder what he's done with all the silver and gold?"

"I was thinking the same thing," Donai agreed. "And did you notice the threadbare cloak of his servant, Gehazi? You would think the assistant to such a renowned healer would at least dress with greater care. I won't be surprised if this man turns out to be a fraud. But I must confess I'm curious to see what he'll do."

"Sh-h! Someone's coming to the door," whispered Ethan, bracing himself against the moment when he would have to look upon the man whose name he had hated for so long. At the same time he felt his eyes drawn irresistibly to the spot where the prophet would appear.

The caravan was quiet. Everyone waited breathlessly for the appearance of the man upon whom the hopes of not only Naaman but all Syria were centered. No one knew what to expect, but they sensed that the most important moment of their entire journey had arrived.

When the door swung open, excitement rippled through the crowd. Then with open mouths they stared at the figure standing before them. It was Gehazi.

"What's wrong? Where's Elisha?" thought Ethan. "If this is going to be another disappointment for Naaman, then I hate to think what may happen. Elisha knew we were coming. Why isn't he here? Or if he is in the house, why does he insult the general by sending his servant? By Baal and Rimmon and all the gods of Syria, Naaman is not going to like this."

A stony silence greeted Gehazi as he bowed and said, "Hear, O Naaman, captain of the host of Syria, what Elisha the prophet saith unto thee: 'Go and wash in Jordan seven times, and thy flesh shall come again to thee, and thou shalt be clean.'"

Ethan noticed a heavy red flush flooding the pale face of Naaman. The general had difficulty controlling his voice when he spoke. "Is that all the prophet has to say?"

"That is all, most honorable Naaman."

Gehazi waited briefly for a reply, but none came. Then he bowed again and disappeared inside the house.

Naaman's temper had finally reached the breaking point. Hope of healing had given him endurance throughout the wearisome journey from Syria. His training as a military leader and statesman had helped him control his anger over King Joram's conduct the day before. Now he felt that even the prophet had let him down. This was the end—the end of the road, the end of his hopes, and the end of his patience. His eyes flashed with fury, and his whole frame shook.

"So this is the way they treat visitors in this land! First

the king, and now the prophet! I thought he would at least come out to see me himself. I thought he would stand and call on the name of the Lord his God, and move his hand up and down over the place of my sickness, and heal my leprosy. Now he tells me to go and wash in that muddy little Jordan! It's an insult to my dignity. Are not Abana and Pharpar, rivers of Damascus, better than all the waters of Israel? May I not wash in them and be clean?"

Naaman's soldiers nodded their heads in agreement.

"These people are trying to humiliate me before all Israel and Syria!" the general shouted. "They haven't heard the last of this! I, Naaman, the captain of the host of Benhadad, king of Syria, will not soon forget this kind of treatment. Mount up! We are returning home at once."

He signaled to the charioteer, turned, and started down the road in a rage. The caravan followed in silence. No one dared interrupt his master's black mood as he sat there in his chariot, staring darkly ahead. Everyone was lost in his own thoughts, and they were not happy ones.

"What a shame!" mused Ethan. "He came all this way and went to all that trouble. Now he's going home to die. What will Deborah think? She was so sure the prophet could heal him. Poor Deborah, she'll be terribly disappointed. Maybe she'll be punished because Naaman made the journey for nothing. I wonder what would have happened if Naaman had tried this strange remedy the prophet suggested. 'Wash in Jordan seven times.' It really doesn't sound hard to do!"

For a moment the boy forgot about himself and his own hopes of freedom. He glanced at his master, Captain Hadad, riding beside him, looking downcast and dejected. Before Ethan realized what was happening, he said, "Captain Hadad, you are very devoted to our lord Naaman, aren't you?"

The captain looked at Ethan in amazement. A slave speaking to his master before being spoken to! This was unheard of. But he recognized the sincere concern in the boy's voice, and he decided that anyone might easily forget his manners under the strain of recent events.

"Of course I'm devoted to him. He's my best friend. Why do you ask?" he replied curtly.

"Master, could you not speak to our lord Naaman and try to get him to do what the prophet said? It's such a simple thing. We'll have to cross the Jordan on our way back. Surely no harm could come to the general from dipping himself in the water. And there's always a chance the prophet was speaking the truth."

"Boy, I've been thinking the same thing myself! I'll consult with Captain Hazael. Our lord Naaman has a violent temper, but when he's had time to cool down, he may be willing to listen to reason. The fact that you were thinking about this at the same time I did is a good omen. If we succeed, you'll not be without reward."

Captain Hadad spurred his horse forward to discuss the idea with his friend.

Ethan grinned to himself. "I have another reward in mind," he murmured, "but I don't intend to tell my master about it. Freedom will be my reward. I'll find it my own way, and soon!"

10

The Waters of the Jordan

The caravan halted by a shaded well so that the people and animals might get a drink and rest awhile under the palm trees. The two younger captains went to Naaman's chariot. The general's face was marked with suffering and despair now, rather than rage.

Captain Hadad came right to the point. "My lord Naaman, you have been like a father to me. Now I beg you, listen with favor while I speak to you as a son. My devotion to you does not permit me to be silent. If the prophet had bidden you do some great thing, would you not have done it? How much easier it is then, when he says to you, 'Wash and be clean'?"

"The Jordan is only a few miles from here," added Hazael. "Please, sir, don't return to Damascus without trying the prophet's remedy. What do you have to lose?"

"What do I have to lose?" Naaman stared defiantly at them. "My pride and my dignity—that's what I have to lose. Why didn't the prophet come out to see me and heal me with a touch of his hand or with some magic saying? As I said before, Abana and Pharpar are better than all the waters of Israel. I shall wash in them and be clean."

"But, sir," suggested Hadad, "you have washed in those rivers already, and they did nothing for you. Maybe when you seek help from the God of Israel, you shall have to do things His way and not in your own way anymore."

"After all, most honorable Naaman," added Hazael, "if the prophet had told you to climb a mountain on your hands and knees, or make a pilgrimage, or cut yourself with knives until your blood poured on the ground, wouldn't you have done all these to obtain healing? To wash in the Jordan is a simple thing, my lord. Do not return to Damascus to die! Is pride more important than life?"

Naaman hesitated.

Hadad brought out another argument. "What would your wife, Shelomith, say if she were here?"

Naaman covered his face with his bandaged hands. He recalled Shelomith's pleading voice and the tears in her eyes when she said, "Please, my beloved, this is our only chance!"

"Wash and be clean!" they heard him murmur. "Wash and be clean. . . . Is that all?"

He jumped up. "I will do it! Give orders to take the shortest road to the River Jordan. Now we shall see if the God of Israel is mighty to heal even a leper!"

"When I get to be an old man, I'll still remember this scene," thought Ethan. He was looking down from his position on the riverbank to where the Jordan flowed, swift and muddy, between the willows fringing its swirling waters. The sun, shining in its full glory in the western sky, had witnessed many a stirring spectacle on the banks of the ancient river, but scarcely any more strange than this. The heavily laden camels were resting; the horses grazed in a nearby meadow. Servants, soldiers, and officers in their colorful Syrian garb stood in silence along the sides of the river, looking intently at Naaman.

The captain of King Benhadad's armies, a man famous and feared throughout all the lands of the east, had stripped himself and was stepping down into a quiet pool of water formed in a bend of the river. For most of the onlookers it was the first time they had had an opportunity to see how the scourge of leprosy had ravaged their commander. They noted with horror and pity the missing fingers and toes and the roughness of his skin.

"He is doomed to death if the river fails to heal him," whispered Donai, the physician.

"Maybe something will happen," replied Ethan. "Sh-h! Look! He's praying."

The silence on shore grew more intense while the men watched Naaman lifting his eyes and his disfigured hands to heaven in a gesture of pleading. Then he dipped himself quickly in the stream.

"He looks the same as before," murmured Hazael.

"Never mind. The prophet said *seven* times," Hadad reminded him.

Ethan held his breath. Once, twice, three times, Naaman went under the water and came up again with no visible results. His face was calm. No one spoke now, and the rippling of the water and the twittering of the birds in the willow bushes were the only sounds to be heard.

Four, five, six times! The silence became unbearable. Some of the men covered their eyes. Ethan stared breathlessly at Naaman's dripping body. The boy's heart pounded against his ribs. There was a strange feeling of fate in the air, as if something was being decided for all time.

Seven! A thunderous shout went up from the men on the riverbank. Ethan found himself jumping up and down and waving his hands in wild excitement.

"He is healed! He is healed! Look at him! Our lord Naaman is healed!"

Naaman stood there in the pool, with water trickling from his hair down over his shoulders and arms. He raised his hands and gazed at his new fingertips, sound and whole. He lifted his feet out of the stream and examined his toes, all in place, all perfectly formed. He felt his skin where the rough places had been. His entire body was pink and glowing with health, like that of a little child. All pain, all signs of disease, had disappeared.

Naaman lifted his arms toward the sky, rejoicing in the new strength flowing through every muscle, a current of life stronger and swifter than that of the river in which he stood. "I'm clean!" he shouted in a voice no one there would ever forget. "I'm clean! O Lord God of Israel, Thou hast made me clean!"

He waded to the riverbank with firm strides and fell on his face onto the grass. Thus he remained in prayer for many minutes. Then he rose. A servant flung a cloak around him. Hadad, Hazael, and the other officers pressed close to shake his hand and feel his skin and express their happiness. Joyous excitement ran through the encampment like a wave of fire.

"Let the men have a feast tonight," commanded Naaman. "This is a time to celebrate. Tomorrow I shall return to see the prophet Elisha and pay my respects in humble gratitude."

It was night. The full moon rising over the hills east of the Jordan shed a radiant light on the Syrian encampment on the riverbank. Fires flickered here and there under the willow trees, showing where Naaman's servants were gathered in groups, resting after the feast and talking in awed tones about the mighty power of the God of Israel. Because of the large treasure of silver and gold carried by the camels, a strong guard was posted around the camp to protect against possible attacks by robbers.

"Or to keep any of us from escaping with a few shekels," thought Ethan. He had finished his evening duties in Captain Hadad's tent, and now he stepped out into the weird pattern of moonlight and shadows woven by the tossing trees. Wrapping his cloak around him, he lay down in his usual place in front of the tent entrance. But sleep would not come.

Ethan had seen a miracle happen that day, and he knew he could never be quite the same again. Now, after the excitement and the celebration had subsided, he had time to think of what it all meant. There had been a Power and a Presence there by the river in the quiet afternoon, Something or Someone that no one could see. But they had been able to see what this Power did for Naaman. There was proof, as clear and forceful as anyone could ask for. There could be no doubt about that.

"It is true, then," Ethan thought, "that the Lord God of Israel is mightier than all other gods. Maybe it is true, too, what Deborah always says, that the Lord is the only God. She asked me to wait until after Naaman was healed to make up my mind which God to serve. Now I can't deny that the God of Israel is the true God, the living God. Yet I'm not sure I want to serve Him or any other god. I want my freedom! I want no god or man to tell me what to do and where to go. Tomorrow we go back to Samaria to see the prophet. That gives me another chance to run away, for the city is a good place in which to disappear. This time I must not fail."

Plotting his escape and wondering where to find a hiding place, Ethan finally fell into an uneasy sleep full of confusing dreams.

In a nearby tent lay another man, still awake. Naaman's

heart was throbbing so wildly with joy and the blood was rushing through his veins with such new vigor that he felt no need for rest.

"It is as if I have never been tired or known pain," he thought. "Even the memory of suffering is gone. What a wonderful God this God of Israel is! It is true what the maid Deborah said to Shelomith. This God is not only the God of Israel, He is the God of the whole world. He is the living God. He shall be my God. I shall serve Him and Him only as long as He gives me life."

Peace filled Naaman's soul as he closed his eyes and gave himself up to the untroubled slumber of true belief at last.

11
God's Gift Is Free

Once more the Syrian expedition halted outside Elisha's home. What a different picture they presented this time compared with their first visit. Then they had been gloomy and downcast, their leader Naaman a doomed man. Without hope and without healing, they had left in a flurry of wrath and angry words. Now they returned with singing and laughter under the leadership of a new Naaman who glowed with health and vigor and came bringing gifts of gratitude.

Two men were standing in the doorway as though they had been expecting the visitors.

"This time Gehazi is not alone," whispered Donai to Ethan. "That other man must be the prophet Elisha himself."

Ethan stared at the man whose name he had hated for so long. He saw a middle-aged man of medium height, slight of build, with a bald head and soft gray beard. His brown eyes were kind, and his face would have looked almost too gentle had it not been for the firm lines of his mouth and chin.

"So this is Elisha!" Ethan thought. "It's strange. After all this time I see him, but I can't hate him. He doesn't look like a man one can hate. He looks like a good man, a man who can talk with God and do things for God, like healing Naaman. So Deborah was right again. It was God Himself who had to punish the young men that time at Bethel. And who am I to question a God who can do what I saw in the waters of Jordan?"

"Before the miracle happened, I imagined him to be a fraud," thought Donai. "Now I see a man with the hands of a healer and the feet of a soldier. He looks as if he does not belong to this world. Those eyes have seen things most men don't even dream of."

"So this is Elisha," thought Naaman as he stepped from his chariot to greet the prophet. "A man of compassion and strength. A man whom God used to set me free from the scourge of leprosy. And to think I almost failed to obey his advice!"

The Syrian officers signaled the servants. The heavy burdens were unloaded from the camels, and a long line of slaves began carrying the bundles of silver, gold, and fine clothing to lay at the feet of the prophet.

Ethan watched the men who faced each other for a moment without speaking. There stood Elisha in his simple garments, with a glow about him which radiated power and peace from within. There was Naaman in his official robes, once a haughty commander wanting his own way, but now a humble worshiper who had come to pay a debt of gratitude to the man of God.

Naaman spoke first, his voice vibrant with joy and thankfulness.

"Behold, O Elisha; now I know that there is no other God in all the earth, but in Israel! Now, therefore, I beg you, take this gift from thy servant."

He motioned to the treasures being brought by his slaves. Ethan glanced at Gehazi, who stood a few paces behind the prophet. Yes, there was the same gleam in the servant's eyes he had seen once before when they met in the city.

Elisha looked at the bundles of silver and gold and smiled. Then he shook his head and stepped forward. "As the Lord liveth," he said, "whose servant I am and before whom I stand, I will receive none of these gifts. Take them back, O Naaman!"

Naaman did not understand. Surely he must have heard wrong! Who would turn down riches like this, the price of a king's ransom?

He stepped closer to the prophet. "I brought these treasures from my own house in Syria," he explained. "My camels have carried them these many miles to give to you in exchange for the gift of my healing. All the wealth of all the kingdoms of the East would not be too great a price to pay for what your God did for me in the waters of the Jordan. I beg of you, accept these as a small token of my gratitude."

"Naaman, your heart is generous," said Elisha. "Your gratefulness is pleasing to the Lord. But the Lord does not desire an offering of silver and gold from you. His gift of healing is free. A heart of love and thankfulness, your life given to Him for His service—these are the gifts He desires. Take your silver and gold, Naaman, and go in peace."

Ethan could not help noticing the changed expression on Gehazi's face. The gleam had vanished from his eyes, and instead there was a scowl of anger and disappointment.

Naaman did not take his eyes off the prophet. Seeing that there was no use pressing his case further, he ordered the slaves to load the bundles back onto the camels. Then he spoke again to Elisha.

"I gladly give my heart and my service to the Lord God of Israel," he said simply. "I shall worship Him, and no other god, for there is none other. But shall there not then, I pray of you, be given to your servant two mules' burden of earth?

I wish to carry this with me to Damascus so that I may erect an altar there to the Lord God of Israel, for your servant will henceforth offer neither burnt offering nor sacrifice unto other gods, but only unto the Lord."

Elisha nodded. "Your slaves may take what soil you wish right here from my own land. My servant, Gehazi, will show them where to dig."

Captain Hadad sent six strong slaves, who followed Gehazi to the back of the house.

Naaman hesitated a moment. "I have one more request, Elisha. Pray for me, that the Lord will pardon your servant in this one matter. When my master, the king of Syria, goes into the temple of Rimmon to worship there, and he leans on my hand, and I bow myself in the house of Rimmon, may the Lord pardon your servant in this thing, as I shall be there only to assist my king."

The prophet raised his hand in benediction. "The Lord knows your heart, Naaman. Go in peace." With these parting words of blessing he turned and went inside his house.

Naaman drew a deep breath. It was hard for him to break the spell of this most important interview of his life. He would have liked to talk longer with the prophet. At the same time, he had a joyous mission ahead of him. All Syria was waiting to learn the outcome of his expedition. What an exciting story he would have to tell! He felt a great urgency to be on his way.

The slaves returned quickly with their sacks of earth and loaded them onto mules. Then the command was given, and once more the caravan set out for the north and home.

"I still can't believe it," confessed Donai to Ethan while they rode along together. "The prophet's house is humble, and his own and his servant's garments look threadbare. Yet he turned down all that silver and gold! He might at least have kept the ten changes of raiment and a few talents of silver. No physician can make a living that way. This man is truly different from any I've seen."

"I know," agreed Ethan. "But I have a feeling that you're not the only one who is thinking the prophet ought to have kept some of the reward. Did you notice the expression on the face of his servant, Gehazi?"

Donai shook his head. "No. What do you mean?" he asked.

Before Ethan could reply, there was a shout from the rear of the camel train.

"Wait, a man is running to catch up with us! It looks like Elisha's servant! Halt!" shouted Captain Hazael.

Ethan reined in his donkey. "I recognize the man. It's Gehazi. What do you suppose this means? I hope nothing has gone wrong."

12

GEHAZI

The whole caravan came to a stop. All eyes turned back toward the figure rapidly approaching them. Gehazi ran with an odd heaving motion, his thin arms clawing the air. His spindly legs covered the ground with amazing swiftness.

"By Rimmon!" exclaimed Donai. "If I didn't know he was a man, my eyes would almost persuade me that I see an ostrich!"

Naaman was somewhat upset at this latest development. Had something happened to Elisha? Had the Lord sent the prophet another message? The Syrian commander was so concerned that he did a very unusual thing. Instead of waiting for Elisha's servant to reach his chariot, he stepped down and went to meet him.

"Is all well?" Naaman shouted anxiously.

Gehazi was at his side in a few more strides. Pausing a moment to catch his breath, he panted, "All is well!"

"Then what brings you here?"

"My master has sent me, saying, 'Behold, even now there have come to me from Mount Ephraim two young men of the sons of the prophets. Give them, I pray you, a talent of silver and two changes of garments.'"

Naaman looked pleased. "It makes me very happy," he replied, "that I can be of service to your master in this matter.

95

Although he wanted none of my gifts for himself, it is fitting that he should desire them to help those in need. But one talent of silver will hardly be enough. Please, Gehazi, take two!"

"My master asked for only one," protested Elisha's servant.

"But he will not refuse the second if it is brought to him," urged Naaman. "Perhaps other young men will come to ask for help. Let your master lay up the extra talent of silver for such a time. My servants shall help carry the silver and the garments to the house of Elisha."

Gehazi bowed deeply to show his consent. "Be it done according to your word, O Naaman. The blessing of the Lord God of Israel be upon you. May He richly reward you."

"My life and my health are all the reward I ask," was Naaman's reply, "and those He has already given me." He turned to his fellow officers. "Captain Hadad, see to it that two talents of silver are packed into two bags, **and** select some slaves to carry these back for our friend Gehazi. Also bring the two changes of garments."

Ethan had been listening with the keenest interest to the exchange of words between Naaman and Gehazi. He noticed the peculiar expression in Gehazi's eyes while he watched the silver being packed and the garments selected. Ethan's earlier suspicion was confirmed.

"Why," he asked himself, "had Gehazi looked so pleased when he thought Naaman was leaving a large reward with Elisha? Why had his face changed to a scowl when the prophet refused the gift? And why the sudden appearance of the two young men from Mount Ephraim at this very moment?

"Something in this makes me suspicious," he murmured.

"Not once during this whole talk has Gehazi looked my lord Naaman straight in the eye. I'd like to find out what's really going on."

Ethan was delighted when Captain Hadad picked him and another slave named Shemal to carry the bundles back to the house. Gehazi took the garments, and the two slaves shouldered the heavy sacks of silver. Gehazi set a brisk pace, and it was difficult to keep up with him.

"Why the hurry, Gehazi?" panted Ethan. "This talent of silver is not a bag of feathers, you know! Surely your master does not expect you to bring a load like this back in the twinkling of an eye."

He stopped and rested the sack on the ground while he wiped the perspiration off his face. Shemal, a big hunk of a man who was used to carrying heavy burdens, grinned and said nothing.

"Your master has been too easy on you if you think this load is too much to handle," answered Gehazi, pawing the ground impatiently with his sandal. "Time is short, I tell you! After all, your own master is eager to be on his way to Syria. I must not delay you too long. There is a hill around the bend in the road, not too far from Elisha's house. You may leave the silver there and return to your caravan. I'll get help from the sons of the prophets to take the sacks to my master's house. Now come, let's be gone."

Ethan hoisted his sack again, and the three resumed walking.

"But will the silver be safe on the hill while you go for help?" asked the boy.

Gehazi glanced at him sharply. Why all these questions? Aloud he said, "There's a watchtower on the hill. We'll leave the sacks there."

So they did. When the bundles of silver had been safely hidden in the ground-floor room of the tower, Gehazi dismissed the two slaves. Then he hurried on to Elisha's house, which sat on the top of the next hill, a short distance away.

Ethan looked back. There was Samaria, the city he had hoped to lose himself in. He hesitated. Should he try it now? If only Shemal had not been along, this would have been the perfect opportunity. But it was too risky to take Shemal into his confidence or even to persuade him to escape too. Two runaway slaves would be much easier to track down than one alone. Besides, with all his muscles, Shemal was slow of wit. A fellow as stupid as he would hinder more than help, Ethan decided.

He sighed. "I just wasn't born under a lucky star," he thought. "Every time I seem to have a good chance to escape, something happens to prevent it. Gehazi might have helped me this time if I had been here by myself. By the way, where did he go?"

Ethan shaded his eyes with his hand and looked back up the road Gehazi had taken. Shemal was becoming uneasy. "Listen, Ethan, we'd better be getting back to the caravan."

"Never mind the caravan. They won't be expecting us for a long time yet. Enjoy a little rest while you can. Hey, come here and look at that fellow Gehazi! He's acting funny."

Gehazi was behaving in rather a peculiar way. He dashed at top speed up the road, then darted into a doorway and hid for a while before making a mad dash to the next door, repeating the procedure.

"He acts as if he doesn't want anyone at the prophet's house to see him coming back." Ethan was puzzled. "See, Shemal; he's not carrying the bundle of garments with him. He said we were to leave only the silver at the watchtower.

There's something wrong here. I'm going to follow him and find out what it is!"

Shemal stared at him. "You can't do that!"

"Why not? When our master sent us with Gehazi, he expected us to go all the way to the prophet's house. Well, that's exactly what I intend to do."

He paused and looked at Shemal's big, dull, drowsy face. An idea flashed in his mind, bright as lightning. "You look tired, Shemal. You wait here until I get back if you want to."

Shemal shrugged. "As you say. What difference does it make to me?" He stretched out on the grass and yawned.

"That's right, Shemal; get some sleep if you can. I won't be long."

Ethan's feet flew up the road. His heart was singing. At last he was free! Here was a perfect excuse to get rid of the other slave's company. Shemal was too stupid to suspect that he might not come back. It should be easy to overtake Gehazi and persuade him to let him hide somewhere until danger was past.

"Especially," said Ethan to himself, "especially if Gehazi is doing something he doesn't want Elisha to know about. I know what he's done, so I can threaten him with telling, and he'll be forced to help me. I must move carefully so that Gehazi doesn't learn yet what my plan is."

It wasn't difficult for the boy to follow Gehazi without being noticed. Elisha's servant was so intent on being un-observed from the house that he did not think about being noticed from behind. By darting into doorways as Gehazi had done, Ethan managed to reach Elisha's house a few moments after Gehazi had entered. The boy heard voices inside and sneaked around to the garden in the back. He crouched low in a grape arbor under the window and listened. There didn't seem to be anybody in the house except the prophet and his servant. "Where were the two sons of the prophets?" he wondered.

Ethan could hear Elisha's voice. It didn't sound as gentle now as when he had spoken to Naaman a short while before.

"Where have you been, Gehazi?" Elisha demanded.

The question made Ethan gasp in surprise, and even more so did Gehazi's reply, "Your servant has been nowhere, Elisha."

There was silence in the room for a moment. Ethan's thoughts were whirling. "Why is Gehazi lying? Why did Elisha ask him where he's been? He himself sent him to ask Naaman for the gifts, didn't he? Or did he? That's it! There are no sons of the prophets here. Gehazi made up the whole story so that he could get some of Naaman's treasure for himself. That's why he had us leave the bundles at the watchtower. What a rascal! I knew he was angry when Elisha refused to accept a reward from Naaman, but I never dreamed he would do a thing like this. Just wait till I see him and threaten to tell Elisha! Ho, ho! I have him in the palm of my hand now! He'll help me escape, or else!"

The prophet broke the silence. There was a choking sound in his voice this time, a tone of sadness and also of anger. Ethan listened breathlessly underneath the window as Elisha said to his faithless servant, "Did not my heart go with you when the Syrian commander stepped down from his chariot to meet you?"

"He already knows it!" thought Ethan in amazement. "But how could he?"

"Is this a time to receive money," continued the prophet, "and to receive garments, and oliveyards, and vineyards, and sheep, and oxen, and menservants, and maidservants?"

There was a ring of something more than human in Elisha's voice, which made cold shivers run up and down Ethan's spine.

"What manner of man is this," he thought, "who can see things happen far away and read the minds of men? Not only does he know that Gehazi went to see Naaman and that he received from him garments and silver, but he also knows what Gehazi was planning to buy with the money. I'd better get away from here before the prophet discovers me and starts reading my mind, too!"

He jumped up, but before he took the first step, he heard something that riveted him to the ground. He was frozen with fear.

Elisha had taken a deep breath. The sadness and the righteous wrath in his voice swelled to a trumpet tone of judgment. "The leprosy therefore of Naaman shall cleave unto you and unto your seed forever!"

There was a moment of silence. Then came a wail from Gehazi, a cry so full of horror and agony that it made Ethan tremble. He ran around the corner of the house just in time to see Gehazi stumble out the door, beating his chest with his hands and screaming, "Unclean! Unclean!"

The boy stared and shuddered at what he saw. From head to foot Gehazi was covered with the telltale spots of leprosy. He had become a leper as white as snow!

13

Ethan's Victory

There was only one conscious thought in Ethan's mind—to get away from Elisha's house as fast as he could. All hope of his own escape from his Syrian masters had vanished. Where could he go in all Samaria, or even in all Israel, for that matter? It was clear that Elisha's God showed the prophet everything that happened. Where could he hide? He had counted on help from Gehazi, a man who was now helpless himself and doomed to despair and death.

"A terrible punishment," murmured Ethan, his teeth chattering with fear. He ran down the road as if a hundred evil spirits were chasing him. "But Gehazi deserved to be punished. He had been serving the prophet for so long, he ought to have known that he could hide nothing from Elisha's eyes. Now what will happen to the moneybags and the clothes?"

He stopped running for a moment to ease the stinging pain in his side from his wild pace. Elisha's house was no longer in sight. He had almost reached the watchtower.

"The silver and the garments belong to Naaman," he reasoned. "Elisha cursed Gehazi with leprosy for taking them. If I leave them here, he might pronounce a curse on me also. We must take them back to the caravan."

He awakened Shemal, who was snoring loudly, and tried

to explain what had happened. At first the big slave's drowsy brain refused to grasp the reason why he had to carry the heavy sack all the way back to his master again. But when he heard the words *curse* and *leprosy* repeated a few times, he realized suddenly that there was danger in delay. Grabbing one of the sacks and the bundle of garments, he wasted no time in following Ethan's instructions.

Naaman listened with mingled feelings to Ethan's story when the two slaves returned to the caravan.

"You have a keen mind, boy," he remarked thoughtfully when the tale was ended. "It was wise of you to act as you did and follow this Gehazi when you suspected him of doing wrong."

Ethan blushed. He knew only too well what the Syrian general would think if he discovered the real reason for his sneaking after Gehazi to Elisha's house.

"You also did right in bringing my property back," continued Naaman. "Captain Hadad, your slave has understanding and judgment beyond his years. Remind me when we get to Damascus that I must reward this boy for what he has done today."

Hadad bowed and motioned for Ethan to mount a donkey and ride by his side. The caravan started on its way again. The story of what had happened to Gehazi spread through the ranks of the soldiers and servants, and the group buzzed with excited talk. Naaman rode for a while in silence, his brow furrowed with serious reflection.

"Don't let this incident make you sad, my captain," said Hadad. "You have every reason to rejoice."

"I'm thinking about Gehazi," replied Naaman. "I know the Lord God of Israel is merciful and gracious, as He has been to me in healing my leprosy. But I find He is also swift to deal justice to the wicked. How could Gehazi be so deceitful? To think that in the prophet's own household there should be a man who did not truly worship God in his actions! It is a sobering thought, Hadad."

The word *deceitful* made Ethan burrow his chin a little farther into the folds of his cloak. He felt far from innocent on this point and still imagined that the piercing eyes of Elisha were looking at him from every direction. And his conscience kept prodding him.

"But I did not really deceive Shemal! I did come back as I said I would. And that time in Samaria, it was true I had been asked to go on an errand for Donai!" he defended, as he tried to silence his conscience.

But it only taunted him right back with, "But you know there was deceitfulness in your heart."

Hadad had been pondering Naaman's remark. "Yes, my lord," he replied, "anyone who serves the Lord God of Israel had better watch his comings and goings, or he will offend and be punished as Gehazi was."

Naaman frowned. "I don't believe all punishment would be the same," he said. "Gehazi's sin was especially offensive to the Lord because he thought he could deceive God Himself, whose Spirit was in the prophet. But is it not true in life, Hadad, that every wrong act carries its own curse, even if it is never discovered and punished openly? And the same is true of every good act. Although it may not be known by others, it carries its own blessing with it for the one who performs it."

Hadad nodded. "A wise saying and true, my lord. I've seen it more than once."

Ethan could not help overhear the conversation, and he thought about it often during the rest of that day's journey.

When camp was pitched that night, Naaman called the two captains, Hadad and Hazael, into counsel.

"Our progress is too slow," he told them. "We've used up more days than I intended, going back and forth from the River Jordan to Samaria. It frets me to think of my wife waiting in Damascus all this time for the news of my healing. The joy in my heart is too great to be held back. I want to share it with her right away. But what can we do with this large caravan of slow camels with their heavy loads? I had hoped to unload them in Samaria and leave the gifts with the prophet. Without their burdens they would have carried us swiftly on our homeward journey. But we can't leave the silver and gold here."

"If it pleases my lord," suggested Hazael, "let a special messenger be sent with the good news. A rider with a fast horse could reach Damascus long before the caravan."

Naaman's eyes lighted up. "Well spoken, Hazael! What do you say, Hadad?"

"I agree with Hazael, sir."

"I should like to ride myself," said Naaman, "but I really should stay with the camel train because of the treasure." He turned to Hadad. "My old and trusted friend, will you go?"

"I consider it a great honor, my lord. When do you wish me to start?"

"As soon as possible. Make your preparations now; then get a few hours' rest. I want you to leave before dawn. Here is gold if you need to replace your horses on the way." He handed him a small goatskin bag.

"As you say, sir. I shall give orders to my armor-bearer. We'll be ready to leave at the appointed time."

Ethan felt no particular enthusiasm when he was told to accompany his master on his special mission. The journey to

Israel had given him many liberties which he did not enjoy in Damascus. Besides, as long as he remained within the borders of his homeland, his hopes for escape were not entirely dead. However, he had no choice in the matter, so he got ready for the ride at once. One of the soldiers was told to exchange his horse for Ethan's donkey. Provisions were packed into the saddlebags. The waterskins were filled, and Ethan saw to it that the horses were well saddled and in good condition to travel fast.

Riding swiftly northward on the main route from Samaria, they left the slow-moving caravan behind and passed through the mountainous region west of the Jordan. At Megiddo the road dipped down into the valley of Jezreel, the ancient highway of tradesmen and armies.

Captain Hadad reined in his horse and halted for a moment to gaze on the valley, peaceful now with its fields of grain and its slopes green with olive groves and vineyards.

"We came through here twice in the past few years," reminisced the officer. "The first time was after the siege of Samaria when King Ahab of Israel routed King Benhadad and thirty-two other kings. The next year Benhadad brought us back to fight right here in the Plain of Jezreel. He was sure he could defeat the Israelites if we fought them on a level place instead of in the hills. But we lost again. It was a horrible slaughter."

"The Lord God helped Israel, because Benhadad said that our God was only a God of the hills and not of the plains," said Ethan, who was familiar with the story.

"That's right. After seeing what your God did for my lord Naaman on this journey, I know now that King Benhadad acted from a lack of understanding. The God of Israel is a God of both hills and plains and rivers and seas. He is the

God of the whole world, and His power is greater than that of any other god. He is everywhere and sees everything."

"The God of Israel did not help King Ahab in his next war with Syria," Ethan reminded his master. "Our army suffered a crushing defeat in the battle of Ramoth-gilead, and Ahab was killed. But then, I've heard that a prophet named Micaiah had told him not to go to war at that time and warned him it would mean his death. And so it was."

"Yes, King Ahab had reason that day to regret that he had spared King Benhadad after the battle of Jezreel," replied Captain Hadad. "I remember how we fled with our king to the city of Aphek, the same town where you and I shall seek shelter tonight. Benhadad was hiding in an inner chamber, hoping to save his life. Some of us dressed in sackcloth and went to meet King Ahab to ask mercy for our king. To our surprise, the two kings met as friends and made a covenant with each other. It was a strange day. But we must be on our way again, lad! We must reach Aphek before the gates are closed. I wouldn't like to have to spend the night in the hills. The robbers are as thick as bats in the mountains by Lake Chinnereth. Let's go!"

It was late twilight before their horses splashed through the waters of the Jordan at the ford south of the lake. With concern Captain Hadad studied the rough terrain ahead. This was the border between Syria and Israel. Even during a time of peace it was a place of unrest, with bands of outlaws waging war on one another and on the passing caravans. With its strong guard of soldiers Naaman's expedition had come through with no trouble on its way south and could probably expect the same freedom on its homeward journey. But two lonely riders like themselves would need to be on constant alert.

"The gates of Aphek will be closed," said Captain Hadad. "But if we can reach the city before it grows too dark, the watchman will let us in when I tell him who I am. My lord Naaman gave me his ring with his seal of office. It will open the gate for us. Spur your horse, lad! Every moment counts now."

Ethan glanced nervously at the shadows gathering in the ravines ahead.

"The road is uphill most of the way on this side of the river, sir," he pointed out. "And the horses are tired after a long day's ride."

He stroked the flanks of his bay mare. Her sides were heaving and flecked with foam.

Captain Hadad gave the whip to his black stallion. "Never mind, we can get new horses in Aphek. Drive them to the limit!"

On they pressed in the deepening darkness, only a few miles from the safety of the citadel in Aphek, the first important garrison town inside Syrian territory.

Suddenly the brooding quiet of the night was filled with threatening shrieks and yells. From their lair in the hills a band of robbers swooped down upon the two travelers.

"Ride, Ethan, ride for your life!" the captain shouted, spurring his horse.

Ethan bent forward over his horse's neck and whispered in her ear, "Come on, run! Run, for death rides at your heels!" He let the whip come down with a swish, and the horse leaped up the road as if she understood.

They reached the top of the hill just ahead of the robbers. A steep slope led down the other side of the ridge and rose again to more hills on the other side.

Captain Hadad waved his arm and yelled, "Follow me!"

In a cloud of dust and rolling stones he rushed his horse down the incline, with Ethan right behind.

The thunder of the horses' hoofs echoed in the narrow ravine. For a moment Ethan could hear nothing else and thought the bandits had stopped pursuit. Maybe in the dark they could not see clearly how many people they were chasing. Could it be they had given up?

No, now their cries of attack sounded again from the hill behind him. Down, down the road the horses flew at a furious pace. Ethan saw Captain Hadad up ahead veer into a small ravine which left the main road at a sharp angle. This was an old trick of war, trying to throw the pursuers off the trail in the dark. There was little hope they could keep ahead of them up another steep hill.

The side trail was rough and twisting, but the two riders did not dare let their horses slacken their speed. Suddenly in the dark Ethan heard a shout from Captain Hadad. He spurred his horse on, only to see the captain's horse stumble over a rock and fall, sending his master flying through the air. A thud, a cry of pain, and silence.

Ethan jumped off his horse and ran to investigate. Hadad's horse appeared only slightly injured, but the captain himself was lying face down among the rocks. Blood ran from his forehead, and he was unconscious.

Quickly Ethan turned him over and bathed his head with water from his goatskin bag. He could hear his master's heart beating faintly, but he did not regain consciousness. Ethan made the injured man as comfortable as possible and led the two horses to a hiding place among some large boulders. The voices and hoofbeats of the robber band swept noisily by on the main road and became lost among the hills farther on. The trick had worked, but it had been costly.

"Is Captain Hadad going to die?" wondered Ethan. "What will I do now?"

For a moment he felt helpless, unable to think of what the next step should be. Then it dawned on him with sudden clarity what his master's misfortune might mean to himself.

"I am free at last, really free!" a voice inside him said. "Nothing could be easier. I can leave my horse here and sneak back across the Jordan while it's still dark. Once I'm back in Israel, no one can prove that I'm an escaped slave, and no one will look for me. Captain Hadad, even if he should live, will think the robbers killed me or carried me off. His bag of gold will provide me with a good living for a long time or even set me up in business. I shall become a trader like my father. This is the chance I've been looking for! No one sees me. No one will know what happened."

He started to undo the moneybag from his master's belt. Captain Hadad groaned, and Ethan became uneasy. There seemed to be another voice trying to whisper to him from somewhere in the still of the night:

"Ethan, what are you doing? Are you going to leave your master here to find certain death? His blood will be on your hands as surely as if you had murdered him. He has always been kind to you. Is this the way to repay him? That money does not belong to you either, Ethan. The Lord told Israel, 'Thou shalt not steal.' You say no one can see you, and no one will know. But God sees you, and God will know. Remember what Naaman said, 'Every wrong act carries its own curse, even if it is never discovered and punished openly.' And have you forgotten Deborah's words on the last day in Damascus, 'Better to be an honest slave than a free man who has to live with guilt and shame'?"

The boy buried his face in his hands.

"What's the matter with me? Why do these things come to my mind? I don't want to spend the rest of my life in slavery! What future is there in that? But I don't want to live all my life knowing I deserted my dying master when I might have saved him. What shall I do?"

He looked up at the stars.

"Can You really see me, God of Israel? Naaman believes You are the only true God. Captain Hadad believes You are more powerful than any other god. I saw Naaman's healing. I saw the curse on Gehazi when he lied and deceived. Deborah says You will help everyone who needs help, and You will bless us if we do the right thing. I know it has worked for her. Will it work for me, too, O Lord God?"

The second voice said, "Try God's way, Ethan, and see if it works. Remember, every good deed carries its own blessing with it. Haven't you found out by this time that only one God is worthy of your worship and your service? Could you be happy fighting against what you know to be right?"

The boy stood up and faced the sky. "I surrender, O God of Israel," he whispered. "I will do what You want me to do, but You must help me."

He wrapped his cloak around Captain Hadad and watched over him the rest of the night. When daylight came, he walked back to the main road and hailed a passing caravan.

An hour later Captain Hadad was in bed in the citadel at Aphek, attended by physicians who assured Ethan that with proper care his master would live, but he would need a long rest.

As soon as the captain regained consciousness, Ethan told him briefly what had happened.

"What are your orders now, sir?" he asked.

Captain Hadad gave the boy a long, searching look. Then

he did what no master would ever do to a slave. He reached for Ethan's hand and held it firmly in his own.

He spoke with great difficulty. "Ride to Damascus and take the news to the king. A soldier from this fortress will ride with you. I'll remain here until my lord Naaman and his escort come through. Go to my house in Damascus and wait for me there."

As Ethan left the citadel, he walked straight and tall. There was a song in his heart. He was still a slave, but for the first time since his capture he felt truly free.

14

FREEDOM

"Deborah!"

"Ethan!"

They stood there in the garden of Naaman's house and stared at each other. After the first greeting an awkward silence hung heavy on the rose-scented air.

"I didn't remember that she was as pretty as this," thought the boy. "In that soft blue cloak and white headdress she looks more like a daughter of the house than a slave."

"My, he has grown tall on this journey," thought Deborah. "He'll soon be a man. His eyes don't have the bitter look they used to have. He is much happier and much more friendly."

Aloud she said, "So you did come back! My mistress just told me the wonderful news about our lord Naaman. She is so happy that she hardly knows what to do with herself. You must be very proud to be the bearer of such an important message."

Ethan squared his shoulders. "I am," he replied, "proud and grateful. When I think of everything that's happened to me since I saw you, it seems like a dream. And now to come back and be received in audience by the king himself!"

"You went to see King Benhadad?"

"Yes, and he gave me this." He pulled a jeweled dagger

113

from his girdle. "See how the stones sparkle in the sunlight! Then he told me to come here to give the news to Mistress Shelomith. He sent two royal chamberlains with me. I have to admit it made me feel pretty important. But to see the joy in Mistress Shelomith's eyes—that was more important than anything else that happened today."

"Maybe the most important part of the whole journey," suggested Deborah.

"No, that was when I saw Naaman cleansed in the waters of the Jordan. Sit down, Deborah, while I tell you the whole story."

She listened with breathless attention as he unfolded the tale of the expedition, from the day they left Damascus until his return. Never had a narrator had a more receptive audience. She groaned with suspense at the incident in King Joram's throne room and sighed with relief at the message from Elisha. She shook her head sadly when told of Naaman's anger and how close he came to not trying the prophet's remedy, and hung on every word when he described the miracle of healing that had taken place on the count of seven.

She sat wide-eyed when told how Elisha refused the general's gift, and how Naaman professed his faith in the God of Israel. The story of Gehazi and his deceit and punishment brought tears to her eyes, and she shuddered as she realized how close to death Ethan and his master had been when the bandits attacked them in the hills. Ethan left out only two things—his own attempts to escape and why he decided to return to Damascus.

When he had finished his report, she drew a long breath. Then she looked at him as if she were trying to read his inmost thoughts.

"You've told me everything that happened, and it's a

story I shall never forget. The Lord God of Israel has heard my prayers and the prayers of my mistress and of our lord Naaman and has healed him in a marvelous way. Now Naaman will worship the true God and even build an altar here in Damascus! But, Ethan, what about you? You haven't said anything about what you think of all the things you saw and heard. Did you try to escape as you said you would? Did you decide you would worship the true God?"

He faced her questioning look without flinching.

"Yes, I tried to escape several times," he admitted. "But something kept me from it every time. Then when I had my best chance for freedom, after Captain Hadad was injured, I couldn't do it. You might say there was something inside me that stopped me the last time. I had learned that the Lord God of Israel is the only God, and I couldn't do such a wicked thing and leave my master there to die."

"Ethan, I'm so happy for you! And you're happy, too, aren't you?—happier than you were before. I could tell the moment I saw you."

He nodded. "It's strange, but after I decided to do what I thought the Lord would want me to do, everything was suddenly different. I don't worry about what will happen to me. As you always said, the Lord will work it out for the best."

She gave him a bright smile. "You remember when I used to tell you the story of Joseph? Now you sound just the way Joseph talked when he said, 'How then can I do this great wickedness, and sin against God?' That's what made you save your master's life. You'll be rewarded, too, as Joseph was."

Ethan laughed. "I don't expect to become prime minister, if that's what you mean. Besides, this good feeling inside of me is enough reward. That, and the way my master looked at me and took my hand when he found out what I had done. But you haven't told me anything about what happened to you while I was away. How are you getting along with Tirzah? Did you win her with kindness as you said you would?"

Deborah's smile vanished. "Tirzah is dead," she said. "She died of fever two weeks ago. We did everything we could for her, but she wasn't as strong as she looked. My mistress let me help nurse her. She told me before she died that she didn't hate me anymore. She said she knew now that Baal was not a true god and that my God was the God to worship. Poor Tirzah! She didn't have a very happy life."

"Deborah! Where are you? The mistress wants you!" It was Atarah calling from inside the house.

Deborah jumped to her feet. "Good-bye, Ethan! It's been good to talk with you. We'll be busy in this house, I can tell you, getting ready for the return of our lord Naaman. What a celebration there'll be! Maybe you will come back soon with your master. I hope so. I must run now!"

She parted the curtains and was gone, like a bluebird on the wing.

Naaman and Shelomith were talking in the upstairs chamber a few days after his return. The celebrations and the parades of victory were over. King Benhadad had held a banquet at the palace in honor of his general, and Naaman had given a feast at his own house for the king, his court, and all the officers of the expedition. Captain Hadad had been there, still pale and shaken from his brush with death, but able to sit up and enjoy the good wishes of his friends. The entire city of Damascus rejoiced over Naaman's triumphant return and his healing almost as much as they had done in the past when he led victorious armies laden with the treasures of war back to the Syrian capital.

Life settled back into its normal pattern again. But Naaman and Shelomith still felt as if they were living in a golden dream, too wonderful to be true. Their happiness over Naaman's healing was increased tenfold by their newfound faith in God. They worshiped every day at the altar which the general had erected in their garden on the soil from Israel. Life was happy and beautiful.

"It was a good day for us when Deborah came to our home," said Shelomith, gazing fondly at her husband, radiant with health.

"Yes, I believe the Lord God directed her here to save my life by her counsel," mused Naaman, "though I will never be able to understand why He should be so merciful to me. Deborah had a mission here in our home, and now that she has done it, we ought to reward her for her faithfulness."

"Of course, Naaman. I shall give her a beautiful gift," agreed Shelomith. She glanced around the luxurious room. "I wonder what the child would like—a new robe maybe, some jewels, or this jar of perfume?"

"My dear," said Naaman gently, "there is nothing in this room precious enough to reward Deborah for what she has done for us. It's because of her that I'm free from my terrible disease and the doom of death. Only one gift is fitting. We must give her back her freedom!"

Shelomith clapped her hands in approval. "What a wonderful idea! She'll live with us like a daughter. We'll give her everything her heart desires."

Naaman took his wife's face between his hands and made her look him straight in the eye. "Shelomith, what do you think Deborah would desire most of all once she has her freedom—clothes and jewels and a fine home here with us, or something worth a great deal more to her?"

She blushed. "I know what you mean. I'll hate to lose her company, for I've grown very fond of her. Still, I know she would want to return to her own parents in the land of Israel. You're right, Naaman. We must let her go. We'll send her back with an armed escort and gifts for herself and her family. How happy she will be when I tell her the news!"

Captain Hadad sent for Ethan. The boy stood respectfully at attention in the chamber where his master was resting on a couch. The captain was still not well enough to return to his duties, but it was merely a matter of time.

"Ethan, I have something to discuss with you. You remember that when you brought the silver and the changes of garments back to our lord Naaman after Gehazi's trickery was discovered, Naaman promised you a reward once we returned home?"

The boy nodded.

"That's a minor matter compared with the reward I had in mind when you urged me to persuade our lord Naaman to dip himself in the Jordan instead of going home in a rage. Then on the way home you saved my life. I'm not unaware of the fact that you could easily have escaped with the gold and left me to die in the wilderness. But you chose to be faithful, even though it meant remaining a slave. I wouldn't be here today if it were not for you. Now, what kind of reward do you think would be fitting for a servant who has done all this?"

"I don't know, sir. But I want to tell you now, Master, that when I brought back the silver and the garments, I was doing it because I was afraid. I thought if I didn't, the curse that came upon Gehazi might come upon me also. I—I really had planned to escape at that time. But my fear kept me from doing so. As for talking to you about getting our lord Naaman to dip in the Jordan, that was nothing. It seemed a shame not to try such a simple thing. But in the hills near Aphek—I was tempted to run away. It was the Lord God of Israel who spoke to me and made me stay."

A little smile that had been flickering in the captain's eyes grew warm and wide and filled his whole face. He held out his hand to the boy as he had done once before in the citadel at Aphek.

"Ethan," he said, "you're not a boy anymore. You've become a man. You're not only faithful, but brave and honest as well. I'll be proud to call you no longer my servant, but my friend!"

Ethan blinked his eyes. He tried to speak, but could find no words. Something glorious and powerful welled up inside him and threatened to burst his chest if he did not get it out. But all that came was a choking sound in his throat. "You mean—you mean——"

"I mean that you're free! See this scroll? It's your certificate of freedom. I signed it just before I called you in. You are your own master and may go where you please. If you'd like to, I'll keep you with me and train you to be an officer. You would make a good one. Or you may return to your home in Israel. Our lord Naaman wishes you to have the two talents of silver and the changes of garments you returned to him. You could set yourself up in business here in Damascus or in Israel. Let me know later what you decide. No, don't thank me! You've earned every bit of it. Go, and may God speed you!"

Captain Hadad sank back on the pillows with the smile still on his face. Ethan bowed and moved from the room like a sleepwalker. Was this true, or was he dreaming?

"I'm free! I'm free!" The echo of his footsteps down the stone corridor seemed to beat out the rhythm of the words. "The Lord God of Israel has done this for me. 'Every good deed carries its own blessing.' So Naaman said once. And the Voice that spoke to me in the wilderness said the same thing. It's true that God's way is the best way. Wait till Deborah hears about this!"

He hesitated. "Deborah! What will she say? She would like to go back to Israel, too; and now I'm the one to go! But I can't leave without telling her good-bye. Besides, I must bring a thank offering to the Lord. When Deborah sees me coming to the altar in the garden, I'll have to tell her the reason I'm there."

He crossed the courtyard and walked slowly down the street, deep in thought.

Deborah was in her favorite perch on the garden wall, gazing toward Mount Hermon's shining crown. She pulled her knees up in front of her and hugged them in wild delight. Tears of joy were still on her cheeks from the news her mistress had just told her. But there was a radiant, excited smile on her face as she murmured, "Home! I'm going home! Mother, Father, Joel, and Ira—I'll see you all again soon! And I'll never have to go away again. Thank You, oh, thank You, Lord God of Israel! Now all my prayers have been answered!"

A thought struck her, sudden and sobering. "What about Ethan? He was so anxious to get his freedom, and now I've got mine! What will he say when he finds out? I can't go without telling him; he'll learn of it anyway. Oh, dear, what shall I do?"

The sound of footsteps in the garden made her turn around. There stood Ethan. His face was grave, but there was a light in his eyes that had never been there before.

"I—I was just thinking about you," she stammered. "Wait till you hear what I have to tell you!"

"Wait till you hear what I have to tell *you!*" he cried. The expression on her face stopped him for a moment. Then something began to dawn on him. His heart leaped.

"All right, you tell me first!" He grinned.

She gasped. Could it possibly be? "No, you tell me first!"

"I'm free! I'm going home!" they shouted in unison.

Deborah tumbled off the wall, and both of them let their pent-up joy explode into such a cascade of happy laughter as had not been heard in the garden of Naaman's house within the memory of those who lived there. Then they joined hands and began dancing round one of the rosebushes until they sank down exhausted on the stone steps and started to chatter excitedly about plans for their homeward journey.

The caravan accompanying Deborah and Ethan had reached the border of Israel. Behind them lay the desert plateau of Syria south of Damascus. Ahead shimmered the Sea of Chinnereth, just north of where the hills parted to make the great rift of the Jordan Valley.

Deborah was riding a donkey which Naaman had given her. She looked back at the distant hills of Syria and at the camels carrying gifts for everyone in her family.

Ethan followed her glance and smiled. "This journey is quite different from the one we made as captives across this same wilderness, remember?"

She nodded. "How could I ever forget! The Lord has been very good to us, Ethan. I was a little sad to leave my lovely mistress, and I know you have some good memories of Damascus, too; but it's wonderful to be going home."

"I'll miss Captain Hadad," admitted Ethan. "He was a good master and a good friend. But you're right. I belong in Israel. It was kind of you to invite me to stay in your home in Jabesh-gilead, since I have no relatives of my own. Are you sure your parents will agree?"

"Of course! They'll take you in like another son. Joel and Ira will treat you like a brother. There is always room at our house for one more. Come on, Ethan! I can hardly wait to see my mother's face when we ride into the courtyard! We'll be the happiest family in Israel tonight!"

"Tonight and forevermore, thanks to God, who led us through our days of slavery and made us free!" He signaled joyously to the camel drivers and soldiers as he led the way down to the land of Israel.